Train the Trainer of the
21st Century

Paul Archer

High House Publishing

First published in Great Britain in 2015 by High House Publishing, High House, Priors Norton, Gloucestershire, GL2 9LS, United Kingdom

Printed and bound in Great Britain by Lulu.com

Copy edited by Shelly Davis

Cover designed by Nirkri

ISBN 978-0-9571738-6-6 (Paperback)

ISBN 978-0-9571738-7-3 (eBook)

For all your train-the-trainer workshops and sales training needs, in-house requirements, contact Paul at

www.traintrainer.co.uk

www.archertraining.com

www.paularcher.com

paul@paularcher.com

+44 (0)1452 730276

This book is dedicated to my family and close friends, for their inspiration and support.

Especially to those who have taught me everything from the world of learning and development, particularly my first training manager Chris Jenkinson, who was an inspiration to me, and Ian Carlton, probably the finest L&D manager I've known.

Table of Contents

The Twenty-first-Century Training Cycle

Here's the traditional training cycle, not far away from what I learnt as a new trainer in 1991.

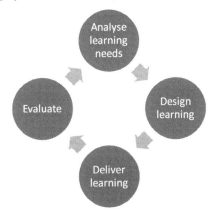

But things change and this is the modern twenty-first-century training cycle:

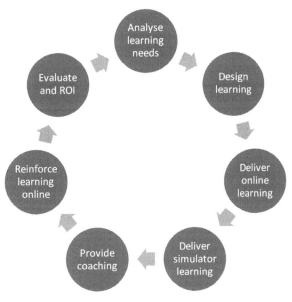

Like it or not, training is moving online and face-to-face training will be confined to running simulation events, mirroring their workplace, and proving an opportunity to develop skills. Coaching will become a necessity rather than an option, and we'll have to continuously drip feed our learners with online reinforcement available at a click of a smartphone and with videos, podcasts, and blogs.

Training changes and I love it…do you?

The Super Trainer

The modern twenty-first-century training professional is a different animal from the twentieth-century one. She has a suit of skills and capabilities beyond delivering exemplary classroom training, presenting, or facilitating. Her delivery skills have been honed so she can present and coach in front of one person, coaching to small groups all the way to large auditoriums of learners.

She has in-depth knowledge of learning theory for workplace adults, learning styles, and methodologies, but more importantly, has the credibility of understanding the business they work in and knowing how their firm makes a profit. She knows that profit is not a banned word and that the firm will naturally use as few resources as possible to achieve its objectives. That's good business.

Experienced in the role and being trained, she understands the politics of their business and is able to influence and persuade business heads. They have the kudos and confidence to meet with the business, have an influencing sphere of key decision makers, and speedily gain the confidence of the business heads who need training for their teams. They speak business language and understand how everyone is measured and targeted. She appreciates KPIs and metrics of every learner she comes across. She can turn a training request into a performance objective and can have conversations that discuss the impact the learning will have on the learner and the business they work in.

She can push back on business heads who think training is the only answer as she has a compete repertoire of business solutions that will help the leader achieve their objectives; many of these are non-training. She quickly turns performance objectives into returns for the business or impact and is able to have a conversation around how we're going to measure the impact and the likely effect on the business – saving or making money. Thus she is adept at working out a Return on Investment (ROI) and showing the impact of their learning work.

The Super Trainer is a learning designer and is an expert in blended learning solutions. She keeps herself up-to-date with the latest learning methods, particularly online learning tools, and continues to reinvent. She can use and produce video; use Rapid eLearning Tools; run interactive web-based meetings, social media forums, blogs, wikis, animation programmes, Prezi, Google Moderator, YouTube, and Vimeo.

She can create simulations, both live online and elearning, giving learners the chance to practice the techniques. She can use Skype and Google Hangouts to coach and is a practiced coach. She can create and moderate discussion forums, online quizzes, and is technically very able and proficient. And above all, she is a practiced classroom facilitator and workshop presenter and paid well.

Eight Principles of Accelerated Learning

Primacy and Recency

Sounds Latin, doesn't it? It means, of course, the beginning of your session and the end of your session. People remember most from these two spots. Research shows that providing real interruptions leads to higher recall as you have more starts and endings. So the magic answer is for us to make more of them.

Here are some suggestions:

- Incorporate energisers during the session to break it up and create a new start.

- Have more mini breaks of, say, four and a half minutes (the half is important as it is unusual and will be remembered).

- Alternatively try 8x45-minute learning sessions rather than our normal 4x90-minute sessions.

Chunking

Sounds awful, this one, and might be something you can get jabs for from the chemist. But it's a really important principle when teaching adults things. Firstly you chunk up and then you chunk down.

Chunking up is where you leave the detail and look at the overall context and principle governing the information you're teaching. You see, people like to see the bigger picture or context and to understand the rules and principles first, and then they can see where the detail fits in. For example, when I'm teaching people about pensions, I'll start by looking at why saving for retirement is vital and some of the key benefits the government grants pensions such as the tax reliefs and fund options. Then I'll go into the detail of each pension product.

Chunking down is the opposite, and this is where we break down a particularly difficult subject into small, bite-sized chunks to enable easy digestion and understanding.

Remember, when designing your content, think chunking, and because the title is unusual, you'll probably recall this one first.

Unfamiliar to familiar

A few years ago a bunch of Americans were held captive, and demands were made of the United States government for their release. The Iranian government, commenting on the situation, said, "The hostage crisis is like an orange where all the juice and goodness has been squeezed out. Let them go."

It's like....I bet you've used this kind of thing before to help people understand something. Make something that appears unfamiliar become more familiar by providing an "it's like". This gives people a connection in their brain which will aid understanding.

A unit trust is like a variety pack of breakfast cereals. For the same price as a big box of one breakfast cereal you get a selection of cereals to enjoy each day. A unit trust gives you a load of shares to invest in.

Here're some ideas to change unfamiliar to familiar:

* Create case studies so people can see how the subject relates to the real world.

* Ask the group for examples of analogies for the subject.

Senses working overtime

A classic XTC number from the '80s and one to get us thinking about all senses learning, which is a cornerstone of accelerated learning. Seeing, hearing, feeling, tasting, and smelling. Think about your content and delivery and ask yourself the question, "Am I involving all the senses here or just one?"

A typical PowerPoint presentation involves hearing only. Arguably they are looking at the slides, but in most cases, they're only reading the words!

Taste and smell senses are cultivated by diehard accelerated learning aficionados who put special sweets on tables and spray smells around the room. Clever stuff really, but not always practical, and you could excite an allergy for someone in your group. The sense of smell and taste has been proven to get to the brain far quicker than the main three senses (sight, sound, touch).

Touch first. When a human touches something it sends millions of signals to the brain and stimulates blood movement around the body. Physical movement does this as well as touching using hands. Research from Nation Training Labs states:

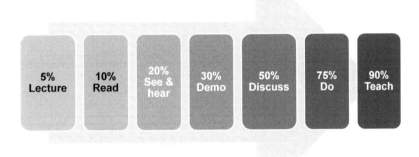

Here're a few ideas:

- Little fiddly toys are great on the table just to get people fiddling.

- Use physical energisers as well as neuro ones.

- Have people pick notes up and touch them as they read.

- Bring in actual props to touch and pass around or samples of the subject you're teaching.

- Get people moving for a purpose, whenever you can.

Seeing. The main competitor to your training courses is not other courses or school…but the TV. Adults get most of their new information these days via the TV, and the telly thrusts out visuals that are really captivating. If you use visuals as well as sounds and hearing, you double the connection to the brain and then the learning happens quicker and stays put. It's like eating sausages and adding tomato sauce. It's still one meal but much tastier. Here's a few more ways of having visual associations:

- Pictures are good on PowerPoint. Print out your slides and pin them to the wall in a random fashion.

- Use the flip chart to draw. Then put your flip sheets on the wall to create wall peripherals.

- Learn to draw cartoons.

- Tell vivid stories which get people to open up their imagination.

Finally, sound or hearing.

Powerful sense and the one traditionally used in adults' learning. The trainer talks and they listen.

Here're some tips:

- Get some voice coaching to make your voice sound more interesting.

- Play music.

- Tell stories.

- Encourage discussion and one-to-one coaching.

Fun

I mentioned earlier about the TV being our fiercest competitor, and good learning programmes on the box use humour. Not slapstick but entertainment. We should do the same. Having a sense of humour helps enormously – it relaxes people, shows our real selves, and shows modesty too. By the way, successful trainers leave their egos in the car when they train people; they don't bring them into the room with them.

Don't be childish, but be childlike in your approach to training. Use fun where appropriate, learn to laugh at yourself, play with toys, and make games to encourage learning.

Children by the age of five have learnt 75% of their total learning. The first five years is vital as every parent would tell you. But how do they do this learning? Predominantly through play and fun.

Distributed Practice

Now this principle is really clever. The basis is that when you remind yourself or practice something you've just learnt, it really begins to stick. The key is to provide regular reviews to the learning at different times and different durations. This has been proven to make the learning stay put. Here are some ideas:

- Provide handouts after the course, maybe twenty-four hours later via email.

- Review each learning session at the end and at the beginning of the next session. Recall the TV makeover programmes, you know, when someone is doing up an old house. Just after the break, the presenter always recaps for us.

- Hold quizzes, tests, etc. to provide a review.

- Start each day reviewing what was learnt.

- Email questions to the members days after the event to stimulate a review.

- Provide a variety of review methods.

- Don't leave it all to the end of the course to review. Honestly, people just want to go home then, and it's a bit late really.

Arouse

Careful with this one, but it does sound interesting, doesn't it? Have I aroused your curiosity? The problem with training sessions is that people's attention dips in the middle. Now you might be providing shorter sessions with more starts and stops, but people's attention will dip somewhere in the middle.

So next time you're designing a session, put the best bit or the most unusual bit right smack in the middle to arouse people's attention. Don't leave the best to last, as we often do; leave it for the middle. Here are a couple of tips:

- Put funny movies connected to the subject in your PowerPoint slides.

- Play a fun game connected to your subject in the middle.

- Just leave the best bit for the middle.

The rhythm is going to get you

Rhythm and rhyme are brilliant methods to enable long-term learning and are great as memory devices. We know dozens of these from our childhood.

- Thirty days has September, April, June, and November, all the…

- Richard of York gave battle in vain (colours of the rainbow – red, orange, yellow, green, blue, indigo, violet)

- Righty tighty, lefty loosey (screws)

- Bid to get rid (unit prices)

Try and incorporate rhythm and rhyme in your learning events. Encourage group members to create their own memory rhymes. Hold small competitions for the best ones. Invent some yourself. Teach people the basics of limericks and let them write a limerick to remember some key points of a subject.

Analysing Learning Needs

Assessing performance

Entry

Your customers will often come to you with a solution in mind. This is dangerous and is where the training field, and you, can get a bad reputation.

It's not a bad thing to be told what training is needed. But what it can do is make it very difficult to measure the impact later on down the line. In fact, it makes this almost impossible.

Entry is about exploring the issues surrounding the need for training. It can take ten minutes on the phone or a series of meetings with your customer – there's no set timescale. But what you need to do is achieve certain results yourself.

What do you need to achieve?

We need to understand the context behind the issues and how resourceful the customer is. This is very important. Get this right and you will shine out in the crowd of training and development consultants.

Here're some questions you can use to get the big picture from the customer.

Business Drivers

- Why is this initiative happening now?
- What/who are the key drivers?
- How important is this?
- What would be the consequences if it fails?

Change Environment

- What is the history of change?
- How effective is the team/organisation at managing change?
- Is there any other kind of change going on?

Structure and Politics

- Who are the key players in this initiative?

- How are they perceived in the organisation?

- How well do they relate to each other?

- How might internal politics affect the issue?

Available Resources - energy, expertise, influence, control.

- Who has it?

- Do they use it?

- Is there enough?

- Can it be released?

We need to find out the resourcefulness of both the customer and their team/department/company. We need to investigate hard resources, such as time and budget, and soft resources, such as capabilities of team members, expertise within the company. This bit is very useful for later on in the cycle when you search for the subject matter expert (SME).

Performance Analysis

If there's a book you want to read over the summer, then it has to be *Analysing Performance Problems* by Robert Mager and Peter Pipe. Marvellous piece of work which forms the basics of what I'm going to tell you about right now.

Before we start, we ought to get one thing straight. What we're doing right now is not a TNA—Training Needs Analysis. This is wrong since using this process automatically infers a need for training. We don't even know what the issue is yet and we're already talking about training. We wouldn't go up to a broken photocopier and say, "Hey, we need a paper need analysis on this photocopier 'cuz the thing has jammed again."

We need to conduct a performance analysis, in other words delve into the performance issue, which maybe…and only maybe…training might be one of the solutions.

This flowchart could help you decide what's needed. It has been adapted from Mager and Pipe – Analysing Performance Problems.

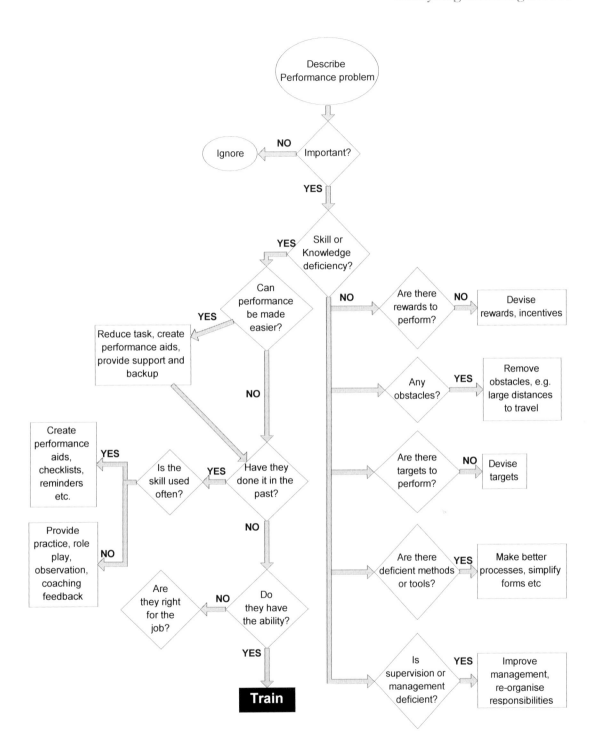

Listing solutions

Next stop is to brainstorm all the solutions that came from the flowchart and your discussions with the customer. Suspend judgment at the moment, then decide which ones have the greatest gain for the least cost and inconvenience.

Audience analysis

Training and development initiatives must, absolutely must be designed with an audience in mind. Even though others may receive the same training, for the sake of your credibility, you must design it for a particular audience.

Subject Matter Expertise

Now you know roughly what you intend to do, i.e., the desired performance and who your target group is going to be, it's time to see what existing material is available. However, you will need local expertise to help you design the solutions. No one person will have all the skills and knowledge for the complete training package. Identify your experts and involve them now.

The Six Steps to a Return on Investment (ROI)

If you ran your own company and you spent money on equipment and assets such as photocopiers, vehicles, manufacturing equipment, you'd want to make sure you could see a return on your investment. You'd hire accountants to work out the numbers to justify the investment in assets and machinery.

Many companies that I work for don't have physical assets; instead they have people who use knowledge to create products and services to make the profits. Okay, they have computers and photocopiers and buildings…but their biggest investment is with their people.

My clients invest heavily in their people, but rarely is this investment ever measured to see what the return is. This is every training professional's Holy Grail – to measure the return on investment to prove to the business how the investment has paid dividends. This will encourage the business to invest further in their people and continue to do so.

It's taken me over twenty-five years as a training professional to finally figure out how to practically do this, and I'm now going to share with you how you can do this in six steps.

1. Figure out the development needs of your people.
2. Show the gaps in your people's development.
3. Determine your performance objective.
4. List your individual learning objectives that let your people perform.
5. See whether the development has worked.

6. Work out the return on investment.

The most important part to the stepped process is the front end – the objectives that you create, and I'll show you how you can do these really effectively so evaluation and return on investment calculations are a doddle.

Figure out the development needs of your people

This can be time-consuming, but if done well, it means you target your investment in the right areas and don't waste money. There're dozens of ways you can do this, but the best way is to empower the managers, your sales managers, to own this.

Easier said than done, and something for another article, but my point is made. Training professionals can do this and often do, but the people close to their people should own the task of determining their people's development areas.

Some ideas:

1. Observations
2. Staff feedback and appraisal results
3. Key performance indicator measures
4. Tests
5. Accident reports
6. New technology
7. New systems and processes
8. Customer feedback and surveys
9. Promotions and position changes

Of course, there are other ways, you can decide these. The important data you need is the gap in performance of your people compared to the targeted performance, in other words, the performance you desire from each and every one of your people.

This gap then has to be shown visually, and the best way to do this is through performance wheels.

Show the gaps in your people's development

A performance wheel is a stout visual representation of someone's performance gap and helps training professionals see clearly where they need to focus their attention and spend their money.

Imagine a wheel with a set number of spokes – each spoke represents a performance skill or knowledge that is needed to do the job.

Here's one I created on a workshop for the role of a trainer:

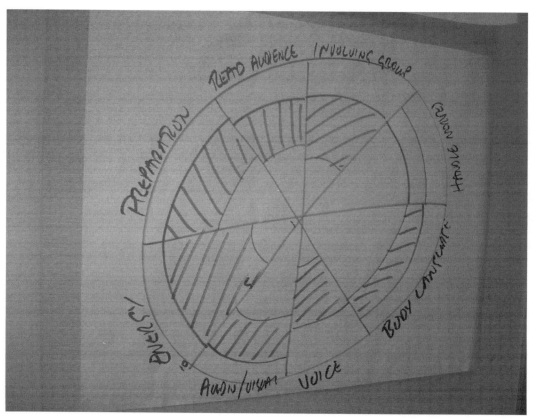

You can see that around the edge we have the skills needed. The wheel rim represents the desired performance of this skill, i.e., the optimum that you need to perform in the role.

This becomes the template for that role. Now you apply the individual people's measures on the wheel, and again, here's one I prepared earlier

Now we have our gap for each skill area, we need to sit down and write a performance objective to stipulate the actual performance needed in this area.

Determine your performance objective

In my view, many trainers miss this part, preferring to dive into the age-old creation of "at the end of the training my delegate will be able to" diatribe.

Instead, decide what the performance actually is first. What's the performance needed, under what conditions, and to what standard? These are your three headings for your template – the performance, the conditions, and the standards.

- Performance
- Conditions
- Standards

Let me give you an obscure example. Say we wanted a performance objective for changing the wheel on a car. Here goes:

You would need to be able to safely replace the damaged tyre with the replacement wheel in the boot of the car within a thirty-minute window. You'd need to be able to do this in the worst possible scenarios – rain, busy roadside, boggy terrain, nighttime.

Now that's a pretty good performance objective. Can you shout, "Watch me do it"? If so, the objective hangs together well. This is the secret ingredient because we can now measure when it can be done simply by watching.

When I've asked people in my courses for their version of the changing tyre objective, most people tell me that they'd just phone their breakdown company!

Next come the traditional learning objectives.

List your individual learning objectives that let your people perform

Learning objectives are the individual parts to the total performance—the smaller, distinct objectives, which can be achieved in turn, often in a classroom, in order to be able to do the grand performance.

This time we need to populate four headings in each template.

- Performance
- Conditions
- Standards
- Assessment

With my example of the tyre change, here's a couple:

To safely jack the car to the required angle, in the safety of a garage using the car's own jack so that the old wheel can be safely removed. This should take less than ten minutes and is to be assessed by your instructor observing the process.

To safely remove the damaged wheel and place away from the scene, in the safety of a garage so it's not in the way and can be quickly placed in the car after the operation. This should take less than three minutes and is to be assessed by your instructor observing the process.

And so on. Naturally you can simplify the language a tad so as not to repeat, but you can see clearly how easy these are to assess during the training course and afterwards in the real world. All you do is remove the conditions from being in a garage to the open road.

These are not far off the old SMART objective setting – specific, measurable, achievable, realistic, and timed. But this new method gives a few advantages and just sounds better.

And more importantly, you can observe them all.

See whether the development has worked

We can also very quickly observe the whole process now by reading out the performance objective and watching them in action. "Can you see me?" is the mantra for performance learning objectives. Once we know the training has worked, made a difference to their performance, we can measure the return on investment.

Work out the return on investment

You don't have to be totally and scientifically accurate here, but you do need a monetary value. Circumstantial evidence of an increase in performance, people enjoying their role more, living the culture, and being politically correct…don't stack up. Yes, they give a warm, cuddly feeling, but they aren't what financial accounting looks for. They look for a return on investment being expressed as money. So here's how to do this part.

$$\frac{\text{Results} - \text{investment}}{\text{investment}} \times 100\%$$

The tricky part is putting a value on the improvement in performance, i.e., the results. Have we saved money? Have we made more money? These tend to be the two questions. Making money is easy enough to establish. Saving it is harder as we have to get prices for the labour or machinery that we've saved. Use the Internet and your judgment, estimate if necessary but get a figure.

$$\frac{£40,000 - £12,000}{£12,000} \times 100\%$$

Gives us an ROI of 230%.

Trainer State of Mind

The Happy Sheet Dilemma

All trainers, speakers, and facilitators have faced the common enemy at the end of their programmes.

The Happy Sheet.

It's a tad naughty of me to call them "the common enemy", but they often cause more harm than good. I know they help us to refresh our trainings, and feedback is the breakfast of champions after all. I'd argue, though, that good trainers will know by mid-morning if things aren't going so well and will change the programme accordingly.

An alternative to Happy Sheets, which I've used before, are your halftime mood checkers. On a flip chart draw three faces – a smiley, a frown, and an unhappy one.

Leave the chart revealed over first break. Around elevenish let the group put ticks next to the smiley that relates to how they feel. You need, of course, to leave the room first. Come back, and within three minutes you'll have your Happy Sheet feedback, but in time to do something about it.

But back to my point.

Why Happy Sheets cause problems

The main harm in Happy Sheets is that they can damage a trainer's Inner Game. You see, many trainers up and down the land have a need to be liked. It's not a bad thing—don't get me wrong—and a need for approval shows we're human. On some occasions this need for approval and to be liked can get the better of trainers, and the Happy Sheets are scanned at the end of the course, and the reader is looking for approval.

At its most extreme, we trainers can get anxious, too attached, needy and desperate for approval and agreement with the group, and try too hard for the group to agree with their trainings, try too hard to sell the topics, and take it very personally when a delegate disagrees with their input.

After all, we're not there to get on their Christmas card list, are we? We're there to help them learn, and if they don't want to, there's not much we can do about it.

Our responsibility to our groups

Our responsibility is quite clear. We create learning environments, train well, prepare everything needed, be an expert in our topic, facilitate well, use the equipment professionally, motivate our group to learn, make it interesting and exciting, but we're not there for approval.

The key is confidence in your topic or skills that you're training. This is vital. I believe that if you are training something, you should be a walking, talking demonstration of excellence in that topic. If you're not, then you shouldn't be training it.

Confidence in your topic will make a difference to your impact with your groups. Search for evidence that you are teaching the right things that will make a difference to the group.

You don't need to convince the group. Be assured that explaining it well and knowing it works is enough. If they don't agree, so be it, but know that it is the right thing, and you know your topic, and it will make a difference.

Don't let your ego get in the way. Be confident, yes, but don't be egotistically so. You're not there to impress. We need to unattached ourselves from the emotions of the event, the neediness this can create.

But we all fall into this trap on occasion, so let me explain how you can deal with this and the rest of your Inner Game when you next need some ideas.

Have I told you before my wife calls me a "bot"? Does anyone know what that means?

The Performance Monitor

The secret is to see where you are lying in the Performance Monitor and to see what you can do to move to a positive position.

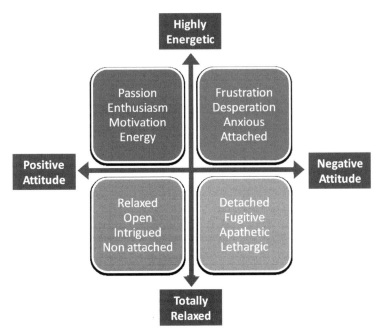

You can see from the Performance Grid that we can be in any one place at any given time, and we will flow backwards and forwards. Know where you are and know how to move if this is appropriate, and I'm going to show you how.

So where should you be? That is very much context-dependent.

The Trainer's Zones explained

Top right – anxious and attached

If I were being chased by a lion, I would hope to be top right – desperate to escape, anxious to live, and attached to surviving. This is commonly known as flight where you'll be pumped up with adrenaline with all the power you need to escape from the danger.

Modern man tends to live here much of the time.

But put me in the same place when I'm training a group, my behaviour is all wrong. I'm desperate for them to "get it", buy into my ideas, anxious for them to take it all "on board", seeking approval, far too attached to the outcome. Not good.

You know the phrase "downward spiral"; this happens here, in this zone.

Bottom right – detached and apathetic

Here we have the same amount of negativity towards the subject, but have little or no concern. If I were sitting in front of the TV watching a totally boring film, that's fine, and I would probably fall asleep. Well, I would anyway.

If I were in a training room in this area of the monitor, I'd better not be training any longer as I won't last long. I have seen it occasionally with trainers, corporate ones who have been doing the same thing for thirty years, no interest anymore.

Top left – energetic and motivated

Now we're in a different zone. We have positivity ripping through our veins, and using our lion analogy from earlier, we now have gallons of adrenaline this time to fight the beast and win. It's the old cliché of fight or flight, and this time we're ready to fight.

It's a good place to be but will tire you out if you're there all the time, exhausting but a good place. As a trainer, this might be a place to be if I were delivering a keynote for forty-five minutes and need high energy, but I couldn't continue it for a two-day programme.

You know the phrase "on a winning streak"; this happens in this zone.

Bottom left – relaxed and open

The last zone is, arguably, where we ought to be most of the time, especially when delivering training. Here we're very positive and relaxed, not too much hopefully. Here we are open and full of intrigue, are receptive, and listen well.

We don't react negatively, are unattached to our topic having to be received well by our groups. We're confident of our topic, know it will make a difference, trust in it, but are not desperate to make sure they accept it.

How to be positive and energetic

Naturally you move around the four zones. Instantly up and down as that's energy-dependent, but very slowly right to left as that takes time, but worth the effort.

Recognise where you are. Be honest. And then do something to move yourself.

I'm now going to show you a number of strategies that you can use straightaway to move yourself from the right side over to the left, where we should be.

Diet

This is often the first place people go to move along the performance grid. Coffee is a primary example. One cup will take you to the top left; two might keep you there, but three will throw you across to the top right.

Likewise, alcohol and comfort eating or guilt food, too much sugar can have the same effect.

But you knew that, didn't you? Life is too short, so let's have a look at longer-lasting strategies.

Exercise

Exercise will put you in the zone, of course. You'll be highly energetic whilst exercising, and the endorphins will rip through your body, giving you an adrenaline rush, which is all good. Whether you'll be on the left or right will depend on how much you're enjoying the exercise.

I've had runs which I've not enjoyed at all and ones I've been on a high. After the exercise, you should relax down to the bottom left, if it's been good for you. By exercise I don't mean just going to the gym during your lunchtime, but a fresh, invigorating walk can have a similar effect.

Breathing

Take a deep breath and exhale slowly. A common enough request when you're facing a highly stressful situation. For those of you who know yoga, breathing properly is fundamental. Chaotic breathing is a recipe for anxiety and apprehension; rhythmic breathing gives you control, prevents front brain lockup, you know, when your brain seems to stop working under stress.

Rhythmic or controlled breathing doesn't stop adrenaline or a fast heart rate, but it will allow you to deal with the situation more controllably and effectively. It stops chaotic beating, which is bad for your stress levels.

So how?

For a man, roughly eight breaths a minute, for a woman, about ten. It's to do with the lung size. Try it now. Breathe in, hold it, and then breathe out slowly. Do this eight or so times a minute, and after a couple of minutes you will have your breathing controlled and out of chaos.

You can do this next time you're in a stressful situation, feeling angry, negative, anxious.

Now this works; you may not believe it, and that's okay. Remember not to get too attached and needy of your approval. Do it; it works. It's like at the end of the day, you get night, and if you sit too long in the sun, you'll get burnt. It works.

Control your self-talk

Mondays are always hectic, especially the morning routine when you just seem to be late for everything. It was freezing cold that November morning and still pitch black outside when I learnt Bethan was having an inset day and wasn't going to school. So I became a babysitter for my ten-year-old daughter, although I had stacks to do that day.

Bethan had the run of the house for the whole day. TV whenever she wanted it, laptops to play on, fridge was all hers, and her two arch enemies – her two older brothers – were safely locked away in school. So I kept my office door open and listened out for her whenever I could. But she was fine.

My day was going very much to plan, and the next item on my "to do" list was a run. I try to go for a run every day or so for forty-five minutes, and since I was going to be working away for a few days this was to be the last run for a while, so I really wanted to do it that day.

How could I leave my daughter on her own at home? But my urge to run got the better of me. Besides, I run along the fields around my house so I was always available, and I thought I'd take my phone just in case. She'd be fine.

I promised Bethan I wouldn't be long and headed off for my run down the lane alongside the house, and turned right across a field right opposite my house. At the bottom of the field I normally stop to do a stretch or two on my aging muscles. From here I can clearly see the house. I looked up and saw, from a distance, Bethan at the front door, waving at me.

Or was she waving for me to return? Was she in trouble? Was she frightened and wanting me to come back home? Thoughts rushed through my mind. What have I done? Poor Bethan, she's in danger. What a terrible daddy I am. I must rush back and rescue her. So I sprinted as fast as my legs would take me.

Gasping for breath at the door, I shouted to see if she was okay. "Of course I'm okay, Daddy. I was just waving at you because I love you."

"But I thought you were in trouble so I came rushing back to see."

"Daddy, it's your fault," said Bethan. "It's your thought."

Later that day on my second attempt at a run, those words resonated with me. Bethan was spot-on. It was totally my fault that I thought that way. I'm in control of my thoughts, no one else, and I chose to think that she was in danger when she was harmlessly waving at me.

You see, we are in control of our thoughts, whether we realise it or not, so next time you're having negative, destructive thoughts that serve no purpose, stop yourself, chuck them out, and control your thinking.

Now before you go and phone Child Line to report me, at least I did worry about her, before my run, and I did sprint back to rescue her!

Anchoring

An anchor is not a nautical term for my purposes today, but a naturally occurring reminder of a state of mind. One of the most famous anchors known to the travel industry is the sick bag. Just the sight of one of these is enough to turn a level-headed and contained stomach into one wrenching with pain and discomfort, so much so that cabin crew don't even mention the sick bag anymore for fear of violently ill passengers.

Around us there are naturally occurring anchors—a piece of music that lifts you, your favourite smell, a taste that brings back childhood, a place with happy memories. All these memories or stimuli bring back a state of mind because they take you back to a time when you first heard the music and tasted the food. The state of mind you had then comes flooding back into your insides and arms you with that state of mind.

For example, a favourite tune for me is Oasis' "Wonderwall" from the (*What's the Story*) *Morning Glory?* album. It won the Brits Award for best album from the last thirty years, so I do have decent taste. A favourite place of mine is Blackpool Sands in Devon where I proposed to my wife.

These are all anchors that help us remember what it was like at the time and relive the emotions and the state of mind we had. To fire these anchors is easy – for "Wonderwall" I play it on my MP3 player or from my phone and the engagement anchor is simply rubbing my wedding ring.

So how's this useful when training people? A lot.

Here's how it works.

Before you next go into a particular event, make a mental note of the kind of resource or state you need to perform well. For example, it might be a big audience presentation or a particularly tricky workshop.

Let's say the big presentation needs confidence and self-assuredness, so let's create an anchor.

1. Step one – recall a time when you had these emotions or states in abundance. Go on, think of a time now.

2. Step two – whizz back into time and associate yourself with the event. Become the person again in your mind's eye. Imagine you are there once again experiencing the moment.

3. Step three – really imagine you're there and relive the experience – concentrate on what you hear around you, what you can see and feel. Relive the moment. Now this will allow the state of mind you had at the time to surge through your body, arming you with the resource needed to carry out a brilliant presentation.

4. Step Four – is some form of reminder or anchor as we call it. You might want to shortcut to this memory again in the future quickly. Just like a shortcut on your computer or speed-dial on your phone, you need an anchor to help you recall it again. Pressing a knuckle is a touch anchor. You could associate a tune to it or a strong visual – it doesn't matter, you choose.

The Trainer's Design Toolbox

What is the toolbox?

Imagine a large toolbox. Next imagine you need to do some DIY. Maybe you have to put up a hanging basket outside. You select the most appropriate tool for the job – probably a high-powered cordless hammer drill (if you have one). If you don't then it's unlikely anything else will do the job, or if it does, it'll take a long time and might cause plenty of pain.

In the same way, we have a facilitator's toolbox. You need to achieve a learning objective. What's the best tool to use? If you don't have a fully stocked toolbox, you'll use the only tool you have available, and that might not do the job properly.

But for us to use these tools, we must first be convinced as to their value in twenty-first-century training.

If it tastes nice, that's a bonus

Weren't the 2012 Olympics fabulous? I'm not talking about the athletes this time but the catering. What a spectacle.

Jan Matthews, head of catering at the Olympics, had a gargantuan task of feeding all the contestants over a two- to three-week period and accomplished an excellent job.

Interviewed by the BBC, she was asked about what she fed them on.

In response she replied, "It's only fuel for them – protein and carbs – but they've told me (the athletes) that if it tastes nice, that's a bonus."

That made me start thinking about training delivery and coaching. We provide fuel, but how tasty is it? Do you make the fuel easy to digest, fun to take in?

Our training methods, are they geared to the learning styles of the learners? How much use are you making of multimedia – podcasts, video clips – that can be consumed on mobile devices as that's the future of online delivery, not boring old computers.

When we coach using GROW (like everyone does), how much opportunity do you give them to speak and discover their own paths? That way they'll do something about it.

Now Jan had a team of 20,000 caterers, and served up fourteen million meals to her customers. Now that's training statistics if you ask me, and every dish was made to taste nice. If she can do it, so can we.

The KAVI Approach to learning

Much has been written recently on the subject of accelerated learning. But does it work? The answer is yes, and we really all ought to be practicing its principles. And I don't mean just bringing in an iPod into the classroom.

This means trainers can use accelerated learning to:

- cover more content in less time and with reduced frustration

- make it easier for delegates to digest content that is complex or theoretical

- make it easier for them to master skills by providing increased opportunity for practice

- increase retention by creating vivid and memorable learning experiences

- facilitate transfer of learning to the job by spending more time on application

The average adult attention span in the passive mode is about twenty minutes. After that, some attempt to stimulate the brain must be made or learners will find it difficult to maintain an optimal state for learning. In other words…they'll fall asleep. But the clever thing is – they do this with their eyes open but partially glazed.

One of the limitations of relying on the lecture as the main method of instruction is that learners remain passive for extended periods. This provides the brain with little stimulation and makes it difficult for participants to maintain the heightened level of alertness that is required for learning.

The major cause of alertness is physical movement. Movement improves mental processing. The part of the human brain involved in bodily movement (the motor cortex) is tucked right next to the part of the brain used for thinking and problem solving.

Now learning doesn't automatically improve by having people stand up, wave their hands in the air, and recite the numbers 1 to 10 in Japanese. It improves by combining physical movement with intellectual activity and using all the senses.

If you ever wanted a succinct definition of accelerated learning, you've just seen it.

It's called KAVI learning—kinaesthetic, auditory, visual, and intellectual.

Kinaesthetic Learning

This means getting physical, tactile, hands-on, using and moving your body when learning. *"If the body ain't movin', the brain ain't groovin'."*

Create learning events where get people up and out of their seats and physically active from time to time. Not all the time, but alternate between physically active and inactive. Everyone likes variety.

Try these ways of increasing the physical side of your session design.

- Getting people to take up roles in a process or system. For example: computer applications, business procedures, the features and benefits of products and sales processes.

- Get people to build a model or process.

- Allow them to create large pictograms or pictures.

- Get them to have a learning experience.

- Do an active learning game or simulation.

- Play a game of snap where a feature and benefit makes a snap.

- Put up a process or map that you want people to learn, and copy it onto a jigsaw for people to put together.

- Take a trip to interview members of the public.

- Create mini exercises for others to complete.

Auditory Learning

Auditory learning has been standard for most cultures since history began. People would talk out loud to each other, tell each other stories and everyone would listen. If you think about it, that is why we use the word history.

Design your sessions so they appeal to the strong auditory learners. Get people to talk about what they're learning. Try these ideas:

- Have them read out loud from manuals.

- Ask them to create their own audiotape of key words, processes, etc.

- Tell stories that have their learning embedded in them.

- Get pairs to tell each other what they've learnt and how they're going to apply it.

- When role playing or acting a simulation, get people to tell you out loud what they're doing.

- Have them create a rhyme or limerick from what they've learnt.

- Get people to talk non-stop about the features of a product. Ask the neighbour to summarise out loud at the end.

Visual Learning

There is more equipment in our brains for processing images than anything else. A picture paints a thousand words. Visual people like to see things, make maps. They like to see colour and shapes and icons.

And I don't mean "death by PowerPoint".

Try these:

- Use picturesque language in your explanations. Make head pictures and use imagination.
- Use vivid graphics in your presentation, such as colour and photographs.
- Bring in three-dimensional objects.
- Go for dramatic body language. Use your arms to gesture, not to hold your hands.
- Tell vivid stories.
- Get them to create pictograms.
- Make job aids with icons and pictures.
- Use mind maps.
- Use room peripherals.

Intellectual Learning

This means what a learner would do in their head to exercise their intelligence to make meanings, connections, discoveries, plans, etc.

It's the reflecting, creating, problem-solving, and meaning-building part.

When a learning exercise, however clever and brilliantly constructed, doesn't stimulate the intellectual side of the brain, the exercise appears as shallow and childish.

Beware of this. This is where most trainers go wrong, and get heavily criticised for it.

Here're some ideas of the activities you can create in your sessions:

- Solving problems
- Analysing experiences
- Doing strategic planning
- Role playing
- Generating ideas
- Formulating questions

- Creating mental models

- Applying new ideas to a job

Visual Aids

A picture paints a thousand words, so the old saying goes. And indeed this is correct. Visuals traditionally come in videos, slides, overhead transparencies, and of course, PowerPoint slides.

This is probably the most famous visual aid of all time, graphically illustrating Napoleon's march to and retreat from Moscow in 1812.

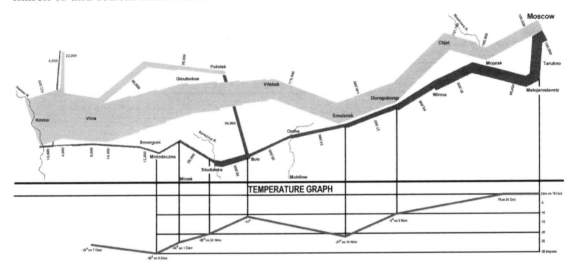

Training with visual aids

Remember, a visual aid is something that is seen by an audience in order to help them reach your objective. In other words, they should not be primarily designed as the trainer's cues.

Two skills you need to use, regardless of media:

AIDS – sets up the visual

TTT – interacts with it

AIDS

- Alert… the audience to what they are about to see.

- Instruct… the audience as to what you want them to notice about the visual.

- Display… the visual.

- Shut up… while they carry out your instruction. Watch to see when they have finished.

TTT

- Touch… the visual to focus the audience on the point you're making.

- Turn… to the audience to regain eye contact.

- Talk… to the audience, not at your visual.

With flip charts this can become write, turn, talk.

With PowerPoint presentations, the "Touch" element can often be built into the design of the visual. More on this later in this chapter.

Peripheral Visuals

Think about it. How many occasions do your learners glance around the room during the course of one day in your workshop? Constantly. So why not pin to the walls various visuals to remind them of what you're teaching? That way they'll subconsciously be reminding themselves of the lessons learnt.

You can produce big colour flip sheets if your budget stretches. Or you can pin your flip sheets that you create during the workshop onto the wall as a constant reminder of what's being covered.

You could pin photographs to the wall of the previous day or large blown-up copies of your PowerPoint visual aids.

YouTube Videos

Hands up, how many trainers use YouTube videos in their lesson plans?

Come on, you've all done it, but are you crystal clear as to the copyright issues? Do you think just because it's on YouTube anyone can play them? Then think again.

This YouTube video will clear it up for you once and for all.

http://clicks.aweber.com/y/ct/?l=Idcfd&m=JgvREMelAkY3N9&b=1GP8jx0bi0lkhdd1Nh iYZw

PowerPoint Presentations

The traditional process to construct a presentation

Recognise this process when you're putting together a presentation:

1. Find an old PowerPoint presentation that worked well.
2. Discard slides that don't fit.
3. Add some new slides.
4. Re-order them into a structure.
5. Decide what narrative to say for each slide.

It's a recipe for a PowerPoint-dominated presentation with you providing additional information, or worse still, narrating the content of the slides. Because they may have a lot of information on them, people ask for copies, and we duly oblige, printing four slides per page. And heavens to Betsy, we might even give them out before the presentation.

During the presentation, you may follow this pattern:

1. Click onto the first slide…talk.
2. Click onto the second slide…talk.
3. Click onto the third slide…talk.

The slides are not visual aids. They are the structure, the points, the content, the lists, the bullets, graphs, maybe some photographs and clipart to make them more visual, but they are essentially…your notes…in the forms of bulleted lists.

You might have the bullet lists animated by coming in from the left, one by one, so you go to:

1. Reveal line…talk.
2. Reveal line…talk.
3. Reveal line…talk.

And substantial research shows this doesn't work. People remember very little of the presentation. Your audience may shut down and hope they don't have to endure any more death by PowerPoints.

I'm sure you're not like that, but you see my point. As a presenter, you deliver your content imperiously, ensuring the audience remembers the content and takes action. You have to battle hard to combat the slides.

But it's still not a visual presentation…it's a presentation with some visual aids. Big difference, so let's look at a way of achieving this.

Here's the new bazaar if you want to have visual presentations, and you may want to make a number of changes to how you plan and prepare your talks.

The new process to construct a visual presentation

1. Set your objectives of the presentation.
2. Select the right method.
3. Organise a presentation structure.
4. Decide the content.
5. Visualise it.
6. Design and animate the slides.
7. Practise.

Let's dive into each one, focussing on your PowerPoint since that's the purpose of this article.

Set your objectives

Not a lot for me to say on this except do it. Consider what your audience really needs to achieve, not what you want to talk about. What do they want to understand? What do they want to be able to do, to commit to, or agree to? Know your audience well and determine the timing. That's the three prongs – objectives, audience, and timing.

Select right method

A stand-up presentation might not be correct. A webinar might be better, a white paper, a telephone conference, a one-to-one.

Organise the structure

I mindmap my presentation structure as this starts my visualisation. You need to become heavily visual shortly, so it's good to start with structure. Standard structure…introduction and gain interest, make your first point, second point, third point, questions, and summary. If it's a sales presentation – state the problem or pain being experienced, your solution with proof, and a call to action.

Decide content

Only include content that they really do need to achieve the objectives, not "filler" or "this might be useful" or this "might add value". Just what they need to achieve the objectives. Then remove 20% of the content.

Now the fun part…

Visualise it

Presenting text on a screen doesn't work. Words alone are not going to cut it as we've already seen; besides, you want to avoid text-only slides with the occasional piece of clipart. Every message can be visualised.

Think about the topic and contemplate how you can turn it into a graphic of some sort. Don't worry about PowerPoint's capability; that'll come later. Just think how you could turn this content into a visual depiction.

Think of a graphic that can be built on screen, animated to grow in front of the audience's eyes. Each click of the mouse does something on the screen, either building, moving, fading, highlighting, zooming in or out, and transitioning from one part of the picture to another.

Maybe it's a photograph to provide a visual depiction. Possibly a pie chart, a Venn diagramme, a pyramid, a map, bar charts.

Describe your message and make it visual. Think of animation or movement, not to distract or to look fancy, but purely to draw the audience's attention to a particular point, to control their focus. The purpose is to control what they see and when, and you talk through each movement or transition.

There's always a picture behind the content and message; you just need to look for it.

Design and animate your slides

Remember, resist worrying about what you think PowerPoint is capable of. You can get someone else to do that. Learn or speak to me, I'll show you. The latest version of PowerPoint can do things that a couple of years ago would have taken armies of Photoshop experts and flash programmers to create.

Templates work well to give consistency of colours, brand, and such. But don't be tethered to the standard bullet lists. We want to get away from those.

Like most busy and frazzled business people you probably only use about 10% of PowerPoint's capability. That's not an insult; it's a fact for many. With some training you can learn:

- Shortcuts, tools, and personalised toolbar setup
- Using media – shapes, charts, photos, SmartArt. Inserting and customising
- Advanced photo formatting
- Animations combinations and precise motion paths – the various static and motion builds available for the slideshow
- Charts and graph animations
- Embedding video and audio

Practise

With all the animation and movement at every click, you'll want to practice a whole lot more because there are no sentences and lists for you to read from. But you wanted a more professional and engaging presentation, didn't you?

Practise so you know what's going on behind you and then practise some more.

You now have a visual presentation, not a presentation with the occasional visual aid.

Twenty-one PowerPoint Tips
1. Talk to your audience, not the screen. Trust the image behind you. Look at the laptop screen in front of you if you have to.
2. Stand centre stage and put the screen off to the side.
3. Place the screen at a slight angle on the left side of the room or stage (and to your right). Adult learning research shows that people use the left-brain to process data, so put PowerPoint words, statistics, and graphs on the audience's left.

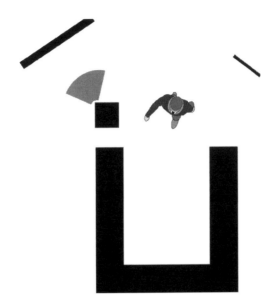

4. Learn to command your equipment. When in 'slideshow', the B key toggles to a blank screen (or W for white) when visuals aren't required. For more navigation tips, click F1.

5. A number followed by ENTER takes you to that slide. Keep a clearly numbered paper copy (nine slides per page) of your presentation so you can be flexible. Use the print command in PowerPoint.

6. Set up your PC so that the left mouse button takes you forward, the right button takes you back a slide.

7. Finish with a blank slide at the end.

8. Put only enough data on each slide to jog your memory. The content should be in your head, not on the slides. Keep it simple.

9. If you have a busy set of slides which you have to use, then create an executive summary set to use whilst presenting and keep the busy set as handouts.

10. Avoid stock templates that just look cheap.

11. Use a wireless remote to give you freedom of movement. Buy the smallest you can and learn to keep it in the centre of your palm so as not to fiddle with it. Alternatively put it in your back pocket when not using.

12. Definitely no fancy movement or sound effects. These are so embarrassing.

13. If you just have to use a busy slide set, then use TTT (touch, turn, talk) to isolate the section you want and maybe adapt a new slide which just shows that section blown up. This way your audience knows that the slide with the detail is still there as a handout.

14. Have each bullet point slide onto the screen one at a time so people can read it quickly and give their attention back to you as you explain it.

15. Summarize charts and graphs that are difficult to understand.

16. Don't clutter the slide - use two slides instead.

17. Use white or yellow letters on a dark background for good contrast. Dark blue is attractive and colourful at the same time.

18. The letters should be no smaller than a 26-point, sans serif font.

19. Use the 1:6:6 rule. One subject, no more than six lines with no more than six words per line.

20. Don't use canned clipart that everyone has seen. Use different clipart collections. Better still, use photos and movies for added interest. But don't clutter the slides with your technical brilliance.

21. If a slide doesn't add value to your message, don't use it.

Prezi – An Alternative to PowerPoint

A study from Internet security firm AVG has found that more children between the ages of two and five can play with a smartphone app than can tie their shoes. The percentages are 19% to 9%.

Fascinating, and our personal anecdotal evidence can prove this. These are children of the digital age, and our very own Generation Y's are well into the workplace now.

So, have you considered how visual your PowerPoints are on your training courses? Do you have photos, images, movement, and visual metaphor sprinkled throughout your PowerPoint? Or do you have text and bullets sprinkled amongst your slides?

Rhetorical question, that last one, but if you have, you might consider using Prezi instead for your visuals.

Prezi is a cloud-based presentation software that can completely visualise your topic. I've been using Prezi now for over three years, and it's really made a difference to some of my presentations and training events.

Try it, www.prezi.com.

Energisers – the Five Secrets to Running Them

Sell them to the group

Everyone needs a reason to do anything, and super trainers are constantly selling or motivating their groups to learn and move onto the next part of their programme. Energisers need even more selling. The reason is that people have built-in barriers towards energisers mainly due to their past experience and pre-conceptions. So how do we get around this? I'll explain.

There's a golden rule in selling when it comes to overcoming objections, and this is to pre-empt the objection by building some pattern in your sales presentation to eliminate the concern before it rears its head.

The same when selling the energiser. Clarify that the next ten minutes will not only be beneficial to your energy levels and you getting to know the group, but I've built in some key messages to enable you to learn the key benefits of motivation or the five steps to cold calling, or whatever you're teaching them.

Connect to the subject in mind

Always choose an energiser that links to the subject in mind. However tentative the link, it doesn't really matter so long as the group get some value from the activity and not just run around the room having a good time.

This is particularly important for pragmatist learners and learners high up the "food chain" in the organisation. Also point out that the active nature of the exercise will help them to learn.

Don't even call them energisers or icebreakers as these have negative associations for many people; call it an activity designed to learn the topic.

Treat them like chocolate

My fourteen-year-old son adores chocolate, laps it up, and gorges on it whenever he has the opportunity. But even he can overdo it. Chocolate is tasty and fulfilling, but too much of it will make you sick. Just ask my son.

In the same way, too many energisers can make the group sick. Not physically, although this can happen, but mentally sick and tired of too many gimmicks. Beware the chocolate connection.

Use them to transition

Microsoft has been heavily criticised over the years for their PowerPoint software programme, which some people adopt with all the bells and whistles available. They have text coming in from all over the place, sounds, and ugly transitions between slides. But good PowerPoint users keep consistency in their transitions so the audience knows when you're moving on to another topic. And good presenters always announce or signpost when they're transitioning.

In the same way you can use carefully thought-through energisers to transition your topics, perhaps choosing energisers that summarise key learnings at the end of a session or introduce key aspects at the beginning of the session. Energisers work well in this cause and provide consistency of approach.

Be clear about your aim

I've seen energisers being used at conferences or seminars where the trainer has obviously lifted the latest one from their book *101 Icebreakers* and have chosen it for no other reason than they liked it. That's fine but, unfortunately, is why they have such a bad reputation from business audiences. I'll show you what I mean.

If you carefully think through what you're trying to do with your group first, then choose an appropriate energiser, this strategy will help you achieve your aims of the entire day, not just a spare twenty minutes of down time or a filler after lunch.

By aims, I mean, do you want the group to:

1. Be more energised physically?
2. Have their brains warmed up?
3. Slow them down for some intensive learning?
4. Individually energise them?

If we plot this on a good old-fashioned management style graph, we'll end up with this.

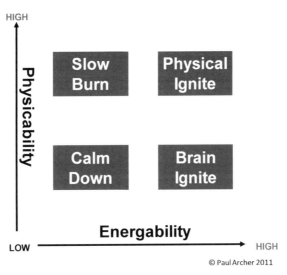

© Paul Archer 2011

You can see that the vertical line shows a low or high physical activity, which I've called physicability, in other words, how physical the activity is, using a dial between using the brain or using the body. The horizontal details a low or high amount of energising or energability. Do you want them to be energised or the opposite?

A low physical and low energising activity will slow the group down. This might be appropriate if they are just too wild. Most of my audiences are sales groups who naturally have a tendency to get overheated, and sometimes we just need to calm them down for some serious learning or a sober message—an individual activity, such as a serious and intelligent quiz where they write the answers down and pass to their neighbour for marking. You could link the questions to the subject, why not, or some other challenging quiz.

A low energy, high physical will give your group a slow burn. Nothing too adventurous but enough just to warm the group up a little. Your activity will be in teams and will involve some physical challenge but not too energetic, such as the nail activity that gets them to stack as many three inch-long nails on top of one nail hammered into a piece of wood.

Moving over to high energising ability, you might want to ignite the brains of individuals, not necessarily their bodies. Here you will opt for the high energising but low physical, such as the 10-Question Brit Quiz or the Premiership Football Quiz, put them into teams and get the flip chart out for the "scores on the doors" marks. Buy some silly toys from the store which all let off different sounds so you can have quick-fire rounds to energise. But don't make them run around in Mike Read style. This is designed to ignite their brains.

Finally we have everyone's favourite, the high-energising and high physical activity games. Liked by trainers but despised by most audiences, honest they are. But they can have the desired effect. Balloons, string, paper, and blindfolds plus plenty of space indoors or outdoors are the raw ingredients for hundreds of different games. Or you can spend thousands on pre-bought activity games sold by many training organisations, ready to run out of the box. Look on my website for forty or so free ideas www.traintrainer.co.uk

Remember, energisers are very useful and help you to achieve the aims of your workshop or conference. Put some time into thinking why you need them, connect them to your topic, sell them rigorously, and you'll never get the rumblings at the back of the room. "Oh no, it's the ice breaker!"

If used correctly, energisers, ice breakers, team games…whatever you want to call them… can bring fabulous value to your event and can even allow further learning as well as the more traditional energising benefits.

Energiser Examples

These are quick tests, quizzes, brain puzzles, and such, which wake up the brain or warm it up after lunch. I love to use them to revitalise a flagging audience. Here's a favourite quiz of mine:

1. How long did the Hundred Years War last?
2. Which country makes Panama hats?
3. From which animal do we get catgut?
4. In which month do Russians celebrate the October Revolution?
5. What is a camel's hair brush made of?
6. The Canary Islands in the Pacific are named after what animal?
7. What was King George VI's first name?
8. What colour is a purple finch?
9. Where are Chinese gooseberries from?
10. What is the colour of the black box in a commercial airplane?

The answers are on the next page. If you want more, there are hundreds of cheap books and magazines you can buy. We also have dozens on our website – www.archertraining.co.uk

1. 116 years
2. Ecuador
3. Sheep and horses
4. November
5. Squirrel fur
6. Dogs
7. Albert
8. Crimson
9. New Zealand
10. Orange, of course

The Twisted Band

Describe how unexpected results can have an impact on learning

This short activity has an element of surprise in its outcome that illustrates how enjoyable learning can be, especially when people discover the answer for themselves.

You'll need flip chart paper cut lengthwise into strips approximately three centimetres wide, one strip for each participant. Newspaper can be used if flip chart paper is unavailable. Pens, scissors, sticky tape.

Give all participants: a strip of paper, some sticky tape, a pen, and a pair of scissors.

Ask them to:

*   Make one twist in the paper strip and then stick the ends together to form a loop.

- Put their pen on the band and draw a line all the way along its centre.

- Ask them what they have found.

- Also ask – if you cut the band down this middle line, how many pieces will it be cut into?

- Tell participants to cut the band and see if their prediction was correct.

- Ask why they think the result was so. By thinking back to drawing the line, participants should realize that the band has only one side.

- Tell participants to cut their band down the middle again. Ask them to guess what the result will be before starting and then to check their prediction by cutting.

The stack of nails

Here's a really neat little energiser that'll get your group perked up ready for a new session. I like it because it's not a majorly physical energiser but will help them to fire up their brain and move their hands and fingers somewhat. The fingers contain millions of sensors that send information straight to the brain to help learning.

It's great for logical thinking, creativity, problem solving, working together. I'll often use it if I'm going to be running a long team exercise as it helps the squad gel.

Prepare the energiser by nipping down to your local hardware store and buying some small pieces of hardwood, about fifteen centimetres long by fifteen centimetres wide and about four to five centimetres deep. Then purchase some fifteen-centimetre nails. Make it a bulk purchase because you'll need a lot of them.

Next, bang one of the nails into the wood but only to about two centimetres. Then you're ready.

The challenge for the teams is to stack as many nails onto the head of the nail in the wood. That's it.

Give clues, if you want to. For example, you could ask them to consider a lattice pork pie. I've seen it done before with over twenty nails.

Remember to explain why you're doing the energiser. Delegates nowadays are much less patient with old-fashioned ice breakers, so make sure they see benefits in tackling the task.

Round Robin

Have you ever wanted to role play something but wanted everyone to be involved? If so, then the Round Robin is a training method that can be used for all sorts of training objectives and involves the whole group and keeps everyone on their toes all the time.

It works by using the U shape of your group and running parts of a sequence with each person in order.

For example, you might be playing the A to Z feature game and ask the first person on your left for a feature beginning with A, the next person a feature beginning with B, and so on. Naturally everyone in the U will be predicting their letter and will be frantically preparing, so do break the order up occasionally to keep them on their toes.

I've used Round Robin to practice the sequence in objection handling where each delegate in turn role plays one part of the sequence. It's worked with the fire escape procedure. I've used it in a GROW coaching sequence training session. Feature, benefit analysis.

In fact, any topic that has a sequence will work.

Put it this way

This activity allows your learners to describe something to different audiences.

So long as you have a product or a topic to describe, this activity will work, and it works even more effectively if the learners have a basic understanding beforehand. It also serves well as an exercise first thing in the morning to pick up on pre-course work.

The idea is that they describe their "topic" to random audiences, which helps them to adapt the topic to different people. As always, sell the session to the group first then get them into teams of three.

Give each person a card with the description of a person on it and ask them, in turn, to describe their topic to each other, ensuring they describe it to your card, not you!

The third person in each team can act as an observer and give feedback on how effectively they described to the person.

You could mix it around so that one person or pair presents to the whole group instead of remaining within their teams. Experiment.

Debrief, as always, and help the group to appreciate that explaining things to different people is an art form and helps you to really understand the technical issues.

Here're some characters:

- Your manager
- A ship's captain
- Someone who keeps asking why
- A child aged six
- A radio interviewer
- Your publisher who wants you to write a book on the subject
- A visitor from outer space
- Someone from nineteenth-century Victorian Britain

Good cop, bad cop

This activity is taken from classic Hollywood crime movies where the prime suspect is being interviewed by two cops. One is bad and stirs the apprehension and nerves from the suspect, whilst the other calms them down to hear the confession.

Using the analogy we introduce doing something incorrectly on purpose before revealing the correct way.

There's a couple of ways to do this—in teams or up at the front.

Up at the front works when you, the trainer, are willing to act out something incorrectly, using humour if you can. Lobby during the break for a volunteer who can act the easy part.

Begin your bad-cop version by doing it really wrong and then pause after a couple of minutes. Move away from the acting and ask the group to tell you what you did wrong and what they would like you to do differently. Continue by doing as they asked to make the process work, but then move onto the next part, this time deliberately getting it wrong. Stop again and invite the group to tell you where you're going wrong again and redo the acting.

You could then launch straight into small-group role play where they continue the role play, ensuring they get it right, of course.

The other way of doing good cop, bad cop is to split the group into teams. Ask each team to prepare both a bad way of doing something and a good way. Ask a random team to present their "wrong" way, then get another group to act the "right" way.

Run the role plays and ensure the contrast between the two is highlighted so the group can see what behaviour is needed in the workplace to get it right.

And it's the right way that brings results, just like the good cop in the movie who manages to extract a confession by being nice.

Stories and Metaphors

I love a story, don't you? I love the detail of a good yarn, one that captures my attention. A thrilling film, a funny report in the newspaper, a snippet from a friend in the pub.

Stories are part of life and very hypnotic. So much so because a good story bypasses the conscious mind and lets us relax and enjoy the lesson. That's why they're good to use in selling and coaching. They work and move people.

And if we see a parallel to our current lives, we spot it immediately; at least our subconscious does and acts accordingly.

You see, that's how we should use stories in selling and coaching. Carefully craft your story, memory, or metaphor to solve the problem of a customer or coachee. Preserve the structure of the problem but change the story.

Here's a story I use to help salespeople bring up the subject of illness insurance for their customers. Enjoy the story and then I'll show you at the end how I crafted it.

"I was on duty, so to speak, refereeing a junior rugby match with my under-twelves one wet and cold Sunday morning. The northerly wind was swirling in over the playing fields; mums and dads with flasks of hot coffee huddled in their overcoats, and onto the field trudged our team.

At age twelve you see all sorts of sizes and shapes in players. Some lads develop early as testosterone kicks in; some fail to grow at all, and that one little lad was Matt, a tiny, slender frame of a boy but refreshingly happy and eager to play every Sunday—always chatty and excited and often the first to the breakdown on the pitch.

After just two minutes the opposition kicked the ball into our half, and Matt, as always, was the first to the ball. Matt only knew one direction…that was forward, and within seconds was surrounded by about six of their players and soon after joined by about six of ours to form a maul.

Pushing and shoving, yanking and pulling, the maul was going nowhere but just before I blew the whistle, the maul collapsed. When mauls collapse, pounds of human flesh and bones pile on top of each other. Poor Matt was on the bottom of the pile and couldn't move. After a short while and a dose of the wet sponge, he was led to the sidelines where he sat bewildered and bruised. He lived to tell the story with no broken bones, but he couldn't get to school the next day or a few days after that.

The next day his dad emailed me to explain that Matt didn't want to play rugby anymore as the bashing and bruising that he got every Sunday was just too much and he was regularly missing school. I hadn't been aware of this until then and I wholeheartedly agreed with his dad's wishes.

Matt was affected by physical bumps and bruises which kept him away from school and ultimately the game of rugby. What about you? If you had some major bumps and knocks, something that kept you off work, how might you cope with a loss of income? Have you thought about that before?"

To craft a story, think of something that's true and has a similar problem within it. Remember the details, the fine points. They make all the difference. Then follow this structure:

1. Set the scene. (Remember my cold, wet Sunday morning refereeing rugby, wind howling…)
2. Introduce the character. (Can you see Matt in your mind's eye, a slight lad with a big smile?)
3. Go on a journey. (Matt caught the ball and headed straight into the group of players.)
4. Have an obstacle to overcome (getting through the maul safely and with the ball).
5. The phrase that pays (how would bashes and bruises affect your ability to earn a living with bills to pay?).

So I challenge you to think of a n or an issue that your customers or coachees might face, an objection you regularly get, and then reach into the deep recesses of your memory and develop a short story you can use to tell a customer or coachee. Then work, try them, and remember to rehearse the story so you get all the details right every time.

The A to Z Activity

I've used this exercise countless times, and it works really well every time.

The whole idea is that the group needs to think of words beginning or ending in the alphabet.

The words they choose need to be connected to the training topic you're covering at the time. For example:

- The skills of a coach
- The steps in buying and selling a house
- The steps in positioning yourself in a sale
- The features of the health insurance policy

If you have two minutes, prepare A to Z on the flip chart and brainstorm with the group, helping them along the way.

If you have fifteen minutes, hand out pre-printed A to Z's and ask teams to write their words on the sheets and paste them alphabetically along the wall. Serves as a useful wall peripheral as well.

The Puppeteer

"We're going to do some fish bowl role play," you announce, and immediately the body language of your group turns negative and you hear grumbling at the back, which you expected.

But wait, there is an alternative, much more fun, and it involves puppets and puppeteers.

Instead of asking two learners to act the role play with everyone watching, you put your group into two teams and ask each team to ask for a volunteer puppet.

Announce that each puppet will be playing the part in the role play shortly but needs to take instructions from their puppeteers. They will be totally controlled by their owners who will tell you what to say, how to act, how to react, etc. Explain that you are an intelligent puppet who can follow good instructions, and you'll be happy to take timeouts at anytime in order to be refreshed and given more instructions.

You can also be replaced if your owners feel the need!

Set the scene and give the teams time to prepare, but not too long because they can timeout as they progress the scene.

If you have a very large group, you could bring in a third team, ensuring you challenge them somehow whilst they're not acting, perhaps observing one of the team and giving feedback.

The Press Conference

This is an effective activity which allows our learners to become inquisitive about a subject or topic that you're training.

Introduce the activity, explaining that we're going to discover the ins and outs of a topic in an interesting manner.

Set the scene. You, the trainer, are the company expert who has been wheeled out into the corridors of power to face the press. Describe the scene further. Explain that in pairs, they are going to attend the press conference to find out as much as they can in order to answer the short quiz that follows.

Simulate the press conference to be as realistic as possible. Have them gather to the front with their pencils and notepads, and you can pick who should ask the first question and so on.

Keep the questions and answers short and sweet, just like a real press conference.

After ten minutes of the conference, reconvene the group into their pairs to prepare for the quiz to see how much they have gleaned from the press conference. Alternatively you could ask pairs to take your telephone call from a customer who wants to know all about the topic. Naturally you're the customer who is going to make the call.

Another way of running this session is less dramatic and involves small numbers of people surrounding the subject matter expert and asking questions in turn.

Mind Mapping

The idea of using Mind Maps has been around for well over three decades now since Tony Buzan created them. They have countless uses, and in training, they can be used in a variety of ways by the trainer to help them formulate ideas for a workshop, to assist their own brainstorming, and to use as notes to help run the sessions.

What is Mind Mapping?

Traditionally, we are taught to make notes, write, and think on paper in a linear fashion. In other words, the lines on the page structure us. Whilst this method may create "good" or "neat" notes, problems do exist using this method:

- It imposes order on thought.
- It imposes a logical sequence.
- It is long-winded and slow.
- It is boring.

- Items are likely to be missed.

If your brain is to relate the information most efficiently, the information must be structured in such a way as to aid thought and recall.

Advantages of Mind Maps

A mind map has a number of advantages over the linear form of note taking.

- The centre with the main idea is more clearly defined.
- The relative importance of each idea is clearly indicated. More important, ideas will be nearer the centre and less important ideas will be nearer the edge.
- The links between the concepts will be immediately recognisable because of their proximity and connection.
- Therefore, recall and review will be both more effective and more rapid.
- The nature of the structure allows for the easy addition of new information without messy scratching out or squeezing in, etc.
- In more creative areas of note making, such as presentation preparation, report writing, etc. the open-ended nature of the map will enable the brain to make new connections more readily.

Mind mapping laws

- Start with a central image - this conjures up creative thought whilst significantly increasing memory.
- Use images throughout the map - (arrows, pictures, develop your own code)!
- Words - PRINTED - for reading back.
- The printed words should be on lines, and each line should be connected to other lines.
- Colour - to enhance memory and stimulate the thought process.
- Write as fast and as freely as possible.
- The basic idea is to print everything that your mind generates and let the map generate more ideas. This method overcomes all the disadvantages of the linear method.

Learners can use them to help them learn and collect information. A quick introduction to how they work can soon get learners mind mapping their own notes instead of writing them in traditional format. Put learners in pairs and ask them to "read" the map – they'll soon get the idea.

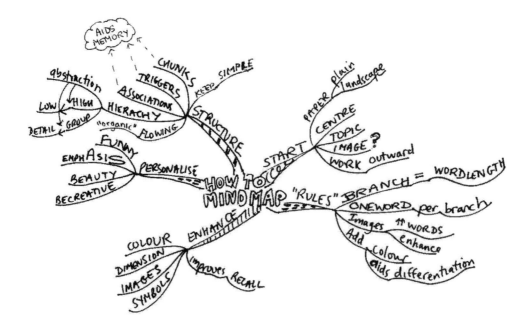

Mind Maps can also be integral to an exercise. For example, say you have a particularly dry process or concept to teach. Get learners to create a Mind Map of the process. I've used them for a variety of dry subjects.

Mind Map Exercise Case Study

When teaching learners about a Code of Conduct (you can't get much drier than this), we asked them to Mind Map the rules but only to draw pictures and graphics. Here's how they turned out:

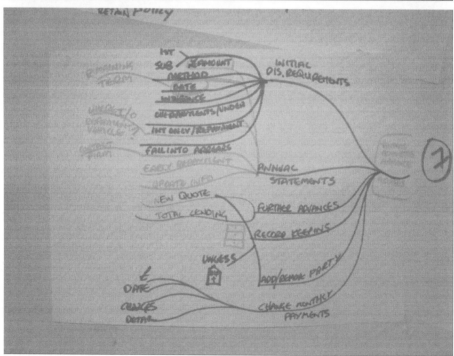

Brainstorms

True brainstorming is a group exercise where ideas flow and are jotted down quickly. You mustn't be tempted to stop the flow.

This way creative thinking is encouraged and lateral ideas formulated.

ARTS to brainstorm

- Ask, provoke ideas, and set a time limit, e.g., five minutes.
- Record all ideas on a flip chart and evaluate at the end.
- Trigger ideas.
- Summarise and regroup ideas in priorities required.

Some brainstorming rules

- Don't be critical of any idea generated.
- Defer judgments to later.
- Go for quantity, not quality, during the brainstorm session.
- Allow your minds to think laterally.
- Use the last idea to generate connected ideas.
- Allow freewheeling and wild ideas.
- Try mind mapping for the note-taking activity.
- Don't discount the wild ideas as these sometimes turn into innovation.
- Appoint a team chairperson and keep it informal.
- Position the team members so they can see and hear each other easily.

Idea Linking

This icebreaker is a great way to generate new ideas.

Bring up an idea where you want the groups' input or ideas. For example, "How do we improve...?" "What's the best way to...."

1. Participants work at table groups. Everyone writes an idea or suggestion on a piece of paper and passes it to the right.
2. Each person reads the idea they received and adds another idea that feeds off it. If they can't think of anything to add, they pass their paper to the right.
3. When a paper has about five ideas, retire it to the centre of the table.

4. The table group analyses all the ideas, and makes a list of their favourite ideas. A group leader writes their top three ideas on a flip chart.

5. The whole group looks at all the flip charts and votes for their favourite ideas to implement.

The envelope brainstorm

1. Put the group into teams equal to the number of subjects you want to brainstorm.

2. Write the subject to brainstorm on a card and place in a large envelope.

3. Give each envelope to each group and give them a couple of minutes to populate the card with their ideas.

4. After a few minutes, blow a whistle and ask them to pass the envelope with the card inside to the next group in a clockwise direction.

5. Now ask the groups to spend two minutes reviewing their new card and adding some new ideas.

6. Repeat until the cards have visited each group.

7. Finally ask each group to present the summary of the cards they are left with.

Runaround

In the 1970s a comedian called Mike Reid had a TV programme where the catchword was "Runaround", pronounced by Mike in his broad London East End accent as "Runaraaannd". He had contestants running all around the stage, and it was a hoot.

This activity is a variation on a multi-choice quiz. Station the large letters A, B, and C around the room. Read out the first question that you prepared earlier or reveal it on the screen. Ask each learner to move over to the position where their letter is stationed.

Read out the correct answer and reward the winning teams.

In their shoes

Here's an activity I've run which helped me to get over the message of stepping into someone else's shoes when building empathy. Everyone knows this so I use this exercise to bring the subject to life and to help people experience stepping into someone else's shoes.

The following need to be dished out to the group, one each. Ask them to answer three questions about the company's product or service (or any topic).

If you were the character picked:

1. What would you think was important about it?

2. What would concern you?

3.   What would have to be done to overcome your concerns?

The characters:

- A customer

- A visitor from MARS

- Someone who is naturally cynical

- A child aged five

- A salesperson

- An expert on the subject

- A teenager like Kevin and Perry

- A harassed parent

- A person in their nineties

- Someone who is naturally bored

It works as a morning icebreaker as well, gets people mixing if you put people in pairs and really funny if you ask people to act out their responses to the questions.

Quizzes and Questions

How to run a quiz to teach a subject

Many trainers run quizzes or tests during their training courses or at the end to help capture learning and events. But have you ever run a quiz to actually teach something from scratch? It works, is fun, and I've done it many times, so let me share with you how you can do it. It works especially well if you wish to teach something quite technical that's contained in a booklet or workbook or textbook.

First of all, you need to decide what you want to cover in your course. And you should have this within a handout or workbook.

Then you announce the quiz to your group. You'll want to explain to the pragmatic ones why you are doing this. They will be thinking a quiz won't teach them anything, but it does. As always, announce instructions in steps, keeping a tight control over the explanation so that everyone is listening.

Next put them into teams. You decide the size and structure of these, but I have often worked with groups of forty people. Teams mustn't be any bigger than four or five.

Then set them the task of designing five or six questions based on the material in front of them. Give them index cards to write the questions on and ensure they appreciate the need for the answers on the reverse of the card. Give them time to create the questions. Suggest they don't go for easy questions.

Put the score cards on the white board or flip chart, clearly laid out, and begin round one.

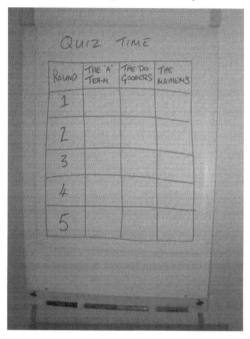

When they have finished, ask them for a team name; encourage cool and funky names, such as the Winners or the Cool Gang, something humorous. Confirm that each team will ask one of their questions to another team and that there'll be four rounds. You have fifteen seconds to determine the right answer, and you can refer to your textbook or brochure during this time. If you are incorrect, then you can allow a bonus to another team worth three marks.

Begin round one. Make it fun and quiz showy. Deduct marks for insolence; award extra marks for smiling, good questions, or because you can.

Keep it moving; do scores after each round; promise a prize; make the event exciting.

After a few times of running your quiz session, you'll collect some good questions so you could have a "Paul Round" to tighten up on the learning objectives.

Give a big prize to the winning team, and as always, debrief the exercise by GLU'ing the whole thing together.

- G – What did you get from the exercise?

- L – What did you learn?

- U – How could you use it in your work?

Don't be afraid to run a quiz session around a particular technical subject. Allocate a good hour; you'll have some fun, and they'll learn a whole lot more than if you forced a dozen PowerPoint slides at them.

Ready-made quiz

Give each learning team half a dozen index cards and ask them to write questions about the subject matter on the card with the answer on the reverse. Collect all the cards and run a quiz along the lines of a quiz show with points and prizes.

Answer search

Ask each learner to write three or more questions on a piece of paper. Ask them to wander around the room and find someone to ask one of their questions. If they know the answer, great. If not, then the pair needs to find someone who does.

The aim is to have all the questions asked. To review ask some learners to read out their questions and confirm the answers.

Question marathon

Put people in pairs. Designate one partner "A" and the other "B". Have "A" ask "B" questions nonstop for five minutes, one question after the other. Questions can be a mix of ones the questioners know the answer to and ones they don't. Have them make notes of the questions neither "A" nor "B" can answer. After the allotted time, have the partners exchange roles. After this exercise the class as a whole, together with the facilitator, can field any questions that remain unanswered.

Question Post

Give learners several large Post-it notes and ask them to write on each one a question they have about the learning material. Ask them to post their questions anonymously on a question board on the wall or on a flip chart. During a break, ask learners to examine the questions and pick off those that they can answer. After the break, have learners read to the class the questions they have picked and give the answers. Learners and the facilitator can add to these answers as appropriate.

Question Ball

Give each person a full sheet of blank paper Ask everyone to write a question that they have on the paper. Ask them to print their question so someone can easily read it and to not sign their name. Have them ball up the paper. You can then collect the question balls in a bucket and redistribute them by throwing one to every person in the class. Or if the group needs a physical energizer, you can ask them to stand up and have a snowball fight with the question balls, seeing how many people they can hit in three seconds. Then, at a signal, ask everyone to pick up a ball, open it, and use any person or resource in the room to help answer the question on it. After a few minutes, ask everyone to read their question to the class and give its answer.

Put all your (question) cards on the table

Distribute blank index cards to learners seated five or six to a table. Ask each learner to write the questions they have about the learning material on the cards, one question per card. Then ask all the people at the table to combine their cards into one deck. Have each table select a dealer. The dealer then shuffles the deck and deals the cards face down to everyone at the table. Each learner in turn reads while you play music. Ask them to keep passing the question cards around the circle to the person on the right. When the music stops, they'll be given one to three minutes to formulate an answer to the question they are holding. They can use any person or resource in the room to help them answer it. Then everyone reads their question and gives its answer.

Hot potato question circle

Ask people to stand and form a circle. Have one of the learners start the play by asking a question and throwing a Koosh ball or other soft ball to anyone in the circle. The person catching the ball has to answer the question. If the person cannot answer the question immediately, they quickly throw the ball like a hot potato to someone else in the circle. The ball keeps circulating until someone can answer the question posed. The person answering the question gets to ask a new question and the process starts all over again. Instead of a Koosh ball, you could use an actual potato. (Variation: To prime the pump, the facilitator can give everyone in the circle a card with a question on it to be asked when it's their turn.)

Team question exchange

Divide the learners into two or more teams. Ask each team to devise a ten- or twenty-question quiz for another team that would test their understanding of the learning material. Teams then exchange question sets. The first team to answer all their questions correctly wins a bag of peanuts or some other prize.

Stump your buddy

In the middle or at the end of a presentation, put people in pairs. Have partners ask each other five questions about the subject matter— both questions they know the answer to and those they don't, If neither partner can answer a question posed, the partners ask this question to the whole group at the end of the exercise.

Pass the hat

Ask everyone to put one or more of their questions on a card and put it in a hat. Then have each learner pull a question from the hat and read it to the class. The first person to answer it correctly gets a point, or a prize. The facilitator answers only those questions that none of the learners can.

Just a Minute

It's late in the afternoon; the group is tired; you need something to lift them, yet you still need to cover some final topics.

Along comes a training game based around the TV Game show *Just a Minute*.

Just a Minute is a BBC Radio 4 radio comedy and television panel game chaired by Nicholas Parsons. Its first transmission on Radio 4 was on 22 December 1967.

The object of the game is for panellists to talk for sixty seconds on a given subject, "without repetition, hesitation, or deviation". Groups of two or three people are given a topic to study, naturally the subject of what you needed to cover in the session. Give them a handout or a weblink if they have iPads or iPhones.

You could choose the same topic for every group but run a number of rounds, with prizes of course.

I've asked other groups to judge whether they do the sixty seconds, and you give them five chances amongst them for each round, until they get good, then you cut this down.

It's a hoot, but do ensure you sell the game to the group to start with, emphasizing that they'll be covering the content in an involving way and having some fun. Assure them that their topics are challenging enough.

Group Discussions

Running a group discussion can be very rewarding and allows learners to put their views across and listen to others in the group, not just the facilitator.

However, they look easy but are tricky to run. Follow these tips and you won't go far wrong.

Discussion Starters

- Syndicate Exercise - splitting the group into smaller teams and posing an open question or a task

- Case Studies - These require small groups to consider a typical situation designed to promote a flow of ideas.

- Brainstorming - a marvellous method of extracting thoughts quickly and excitedly.

- Questions - Use open questions to stimulate the group's thoughts.
- "How do you feel about that?"
- "What do you think would happen if..."
- "Help me to see how this fits with..."
- "Rosemary, you look as if you've got something to say."
- "Mike, you don't feel comfortable with that?"
- Devil's Advocate - useful to trigger ideas from a quiet group

Discussion Lubricators

- Verbal lubricators – "I see", "Aha", "That's interesting!", "Really"
- Non-verbal – nodding, constant eye contact, leaning forward, sitting down

Discussion Controlling

- Regulating - Interrupt long-winded talkers with questions.
- Focusing - Keep the subject in front of the class. Use a flip chart to refocus.
- Guiding - Use reflective questions to guide participants. Add your own points and give examples.
- Interpreting - Rephrase points to assist badly thought-out ideas and to encourage quiet delegates.
- Summarise - List points on the flip chart regularly, and constantly summarise the direction at each logical point.

Discussion Template

1. The discussion topic is:
2. The objectives of the discussion are:
3. The best course to follow in examining the topic is:
4. My introduction to the topic will be:
5. Some constructive questions I might ask are:

Debates

Great when you have a particularly sensitive subject or a topic where you want the group to really tell you their personal opinions.

Classic rules apply.

- You have one team who propose the motion and one team to oppose it.

- You select the motion but be contentious with the title. For example, the house proposes that the penalty fine system should be abolished with immediate effect.

- The teams have time to prepare their arguments.

- They prepare a two-minute presentation pushing their arguments.

- Run the main presentations.

- Each team then must do a thirty-second supplement to their main argument where they may pick up on any arguments proposed during the first round.

- Votes are then taken to decide the winner.

- Run a quick group discussion to bring out the main points of the debate.

- Total running time, twenty minutes.

Role Play and Simulations

Whole, part, whole

When my son was younger, I trained with the English Rugby Union to become a rugby coach. The technique I remember to this day is the concept of whole, part, whole.

Let me explain how this works and how it can help your coaching and training whether you're a sales manager or a trainer.

We began the coaching session with a short game, and the kids loved this because that's what they wanted to do – play rugby. We then paused the game during a certain move, like a scrum or lateral passing, and then did a mini coaching session around that technique. Once they mastered the technique, we resumed the game where they were able to apply the new technique they had just learnt. And when they had more success it was thrilling to see the engagement in the boys' faces.

This is classic and should be the way we train and coach salespeople.

Start with the whole; create the context where the training fits. Provide the context of their job. Then do the skill or technique training, applying it to the context. And finally, fit the new technique into the context once again and see what a difference it makes.

It seems so simple, but I see countless corporate trainers merely pushing information at their learners, no context, just content. This content can be delivered in a variety of ways, but it can become almost indistinguishable from the day-to-day job that the learner does.

So next time you need to train a performance, make sure you articulate what that performance looks like and then operate whole, part, whole. Let me give you an example.

I'm developing some training for a client which involves a sales manager and how they manage their team of salespeople. I'm developing the whole by a "day in the life" of the sales manager. I'm creating a realistic and genuine context, i.e., their office on the start of Wednesday. Then I'm going to create various situations which occur and put them into a position where they have to make some decisions about these situations, how would they handle an unmotivated salesperson, someone whose numbers are down. I'm going to allow them to make decisions, get it wrong, learn by getting it wrong, and ultimately see the enjoyment when they get it right.

Just like my twelve-year-old lads without a worry in the world scoring points because they've just learnt a new technique.

Role playing is a dramatised form of case study in which learners act out an issue under the guidance of the facilitator, who gives an evaluation of the performance in light of previously taught principles.

Role Play

To make role play work:-

• It must be realistic.

• The situation must be one which delegates can identify with.

• Learners must live their parts.

• Facilitators can play the challenging roles, not learners. Or you can splash out on some actors.

Role play either lives or dies with the feedback that is given. Always carry out role play in small groups of no more than three or four. The fish bowl technique which places a delegate right at the front neither serves a purpose nor is any fun for anyone.

Role play and facilitator feedback

- First ask the role players for an "auto-critique".

- Use your probing skills to develop their own thoughts.

- Then ask the group to comment, probing where necessary.

- Add your own critique but:

- Give appropriate praise. Try the "praise sandwich".

- Offer alternatives when commenting.

- Address the individual concerned.

Role play and group feedback

One of my favourite programmes on TV right now is *Come Dine With Me,* a comedy, fly-on-the-wall show of four diners who cook for each other over a period of four days.

This show has a useful technique that we can use in role play.

Let me explain.

If you're training to improve your group's skills, then you have to give them the opportunity to practice. How else can you help them to turn your trainings into a personal skill?

We use role play for this purpose, and yes, everyone has a personal opinion on this under-rated trainer tool. Run properly, it can be a very effective way of developing a skill, especially if you let the group split into smaller groups to undertake the role play isolated from the main group.

That way you ensure smaller groups of a maximum of four people are doing the role play together and giving each other semi-private feedback. That's where my show comes in.

You see, one of the challenges for role play feedback is the individuals take a long time, repeat themselves, when it's better just to move on quickly, so the technique they use on *Come Dine With Me* does work.

After each dinner party, rather inebriated in the taxi home, they vote for their host that night and produce a card with a mark out of ten and have to briefly explain why.

They explain why for a maximum of about fifteen seconds and it's over with in a jiffy.

So give your people cards, numbered one to ten, and ask them to display the card with a number after each role play and explain why. People will be kind, believe me, and don't make it a competition.

But make sure they don't do it inebriated in the taxi on the way home.

Hot seat coaching

An extremely clever yet simple technique which allows the facilitator to interrupt the role play halfway through to provide initial feedback. Armed with the feedback, the leaner can re-start the role play where they finished and improve their performance.

Forum theatre

Forum theatre is a relatively new concept in the field of training and development. Its strength comes by removing the fear that many individuals have with role play. It achieves the same goals as role play but removes much of the vulnerability that people feel they have.

Your learners are shown a short play in which a central character encounters a work-based obstacle or barrier. The play can be any situation based on a work-based scenario or problem that your training course has been designed to provide skills to use.

For example, you might be training assertiveness skills so your play will involve a work situation where some of the characters are going have to stick up for themselves in an assertive manner.

Each of the actors (which can be professional actors or willing volunteers from your learners) is controlled by one or more learners. In this way, they are the directors of the play.

The directors can stop the play at any time to brief their actor, and the play can be rewound to enhance the learning. The directors can take the place of the actor, if they so wish. New characters can be introduced to the scene.

Forum theatre – an example

Recently I used an adaptation of forum theatre during a training course on influencing and persuasion skills, and here's how it worked.

There were twelve learners on the course, so my first step was to bring in some actors. I used actors from the local university.

The learners were split into teams of four and allocated an actor each. They were given the basis of a real-life business situation where influencing and persuasion was needed to be successful. I gave the whole group a brief which they adapted to suit their roles.

Three employees work in an open plan office and find that the position of their desk causes them to get distracted by people walking by. The need was to get the agreement of two colleagues to reposition the desk as this impacts their desk position.

Nothing too dramatic but plenty of scope to use influencing skills.

In their teams of four, they were asked to decide how their actor was going to approach the meeting that was about to happen. They needed to determine what the objective was for their actor and the way that person should approach the meeting and the tactics and methods they would adopt to achieve their goal.

The theatre then began with the three actors playing their parts.

I acted as the "joker", i.e., someone with no allegiance to any cards, and facilitated the event. The play was stopped and restarted after some extra briefing from the directors. Different tactics were tried and reactions witnessed and discussed.

Training Simulations and *Star Trek*

My wife calls me a Trekkie. And yes, I like *Star Trek* – have ever since Captain Kirk slipped into his uniform back in the 1960s.

My favourite is *The Next Generation*, full of new characters, great storylines and one or two new inventions. The Holodeck is one. Let me explain to you one episode that has huge implications for us in training and development.

First Officer Riker had been arrested for murder, and the judge and jury decided to re-enact the whole scene using evidence and information given to the computer, which literally ran the whole event in 3D in front of them. The computer was able to conjure up various versions of the event according to different eyewitness reports, and each version was as lifelike as the rest.

Now that's what you call a simulation.

The judge and jury were able to pause the action, rewind it, and replay certain parts to help with their judgment.

Now in training especially when we're training techniques to help with skill development, we simply have to get into the same level of simulation so our learners can put their new techniques into practice and receive feedback and be able to watch themselves in action.

So the use of simulated role plays takes a completely new and different dimension if we compare them to the Holodeck. Now we don't have this kind of technology at our fingertips, but we do have the ability to create real-world scenarios and simulations. Use actors if you can afford it or the local members of an amateur dramatic society. Film the scene and stream it straight onto the Internet for others to watch and give feedback on. Stop it, pause it, rewind it, and replay scenes that are useful to help in the feedback.

The distant future of training will be using something like the Holodeck – the technology isn't quite there for all of us yet but it's not too far away.

Did First Officer William Riker escape the death penalty and avoid being convicted? Of course he did. First Officer Riker is the hero and a stylish, sophisticated, and handsome chap – but that's *Star Trek*.

Cartooning

If you have ever watched someone drawing you may have found yourself becoming completely absorbed as the picture develops, totally transfixed as you focus on the artist's every move. The effect is "hypnotic" as the audience becomes completely absorbed.

As a presenter, just imagine being able to instantly grab the attention of a group in this way. The ability to draw is a powerful communication device – a picture is worth a thousand words.

So how can you use cartoons? Here're some suggestions:

- As an introduction to a topic
- To help explain a topic and to engage the learners
- Add to mind maps to help learners understand and remember something
- To liven up your flip charts
- Wall peripherals
- To allow learners to express themselves

On the next couple of pages are some examples of cartoon usage on training courses.

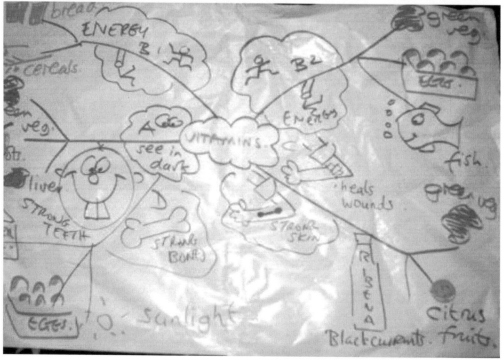

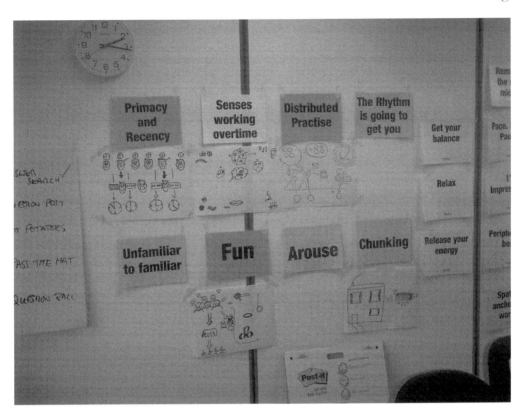

Games and activities

I was watching my six-year-old son the other day, deeply immersed in learning adding and subtracting numbers. He was excited, enthralled, and really making headway. What was he doing? He was not in classroom with a teacher or reading a textbook – he was playing a computer game. It involved bowling hedgehogs down a bowling alley to earn points.

It worked.

It is in the midst of play that we are most in possession of our full powers. An unobstructed sense of play releases all sorts of positive endorphins in our bodies and gives us the sense of being fully alive. Learning games that create a playful atmosphere and release people's full and unbridled intelligence have a contribution to make.

Learning games, wisely used, can:

- take the inhibiting "seriousness" out of the air

- de-stress the learning environment

- get people totally involved

- improve the teaming process

Accelerated Learning does not always require games, and games of themselves do not always accelerate learning, but games used with discretion can add variety, zest, and interest to some learning programs.

A warning

Like all learning techniques, games are not ends in themselves but only means towards the ends of enhanced learning. Sometimes a game can be interesting, clever, fun, and very engaging, but produces no substantial learning or long-term value. In that case it's just a big waste of time and should be scrapped. The simple rule is this: If games result in enhanced learning and improved job performance, use them; if they don't, don't.

Games that add value

In order for a learning game to be effective and add real value to the learning process it should:

- Be related directly to the workplace. The best games are ones that provide knowledge, reinforce attitudes, and initiate action essential for success on the job.

- Teach people how to think, access information, react, understand, grow, and create real-world value for themselves and their organization on a continuing basis.

- Allow for collaboration among learners. (Any competition in a game should be between teams and not individuals.)

- Be challenging, but not to the point of frustration and disconnect.

- Permit ample time for reflection, feedback, dialog, and integration.

And remember this: Don't overdo it! Too much of any one thing (games included) can destroy learning effectiveness.

Picture Framing

The technique is called picture framing and works with frames of 6-12. The idea is that you represent the stages of a process as pictures – one picture per frame.

You can run this activity in a number of ways. You could devise the pictures yourself and issue to groups of learners for them to interpret the meaning.

You can ask them to think of the process that they need to learn. Maybe it's in writing or in a company procedure manual. Allow them in teams to develop their own picture frames with associated descriptions.

Maybe test how good their frames are by giving just the pictures to another team for them to interpret.

Whatever you do, just play around with the concept. Bear in mind, though, that the learning will stick in the minds of the learners more effectively than any other traditional learning.

Case Studies

These methods of learning have been used for many years now as a useful technique to start applying theory to the workplace.

The case study is a situation involving people, places, challenges, timescales, etc. The idea is to allow learners, on their own or in small teams, to explore the situation against the issues, concepts that they are learning. The case study must be real and one which learners will recognise and see in their day-to-day lives, otherwise it becomes training theory.

The best case studies are based on real people (changing the names to protect the innocent) and should have various questions to answer to apply the knowledge being learnt. The trainer can create the case study and write the questions to apply the learning.

The case study questions can be answered by learners, ideally in groups to encourage discussion amongst themselves. The physical act of talking to each other helps to cement the learning.

The questions, once answered, can be discussed amongst the whole group so they are useful lubricators for a group discussion.

Case studies can be drawn from the group, even asked for in pre-course work. That way you can ensure totally accuracy and relevance.

Working with Learners

Now I Know My ABC...and D

How to kick off any presentation with style

I used to love watching *Sesame Street* as a kid. It was an American TV show with Muppet-style puppets. Every episode had some major learning point for us kids, but we loved the programme for its colour, fun, and songs.

One of my favourite songs was the ABC song which ended, "Now I know my ABCs. Next time will you sing with me?"

Now this song always reminds me of the ABCD of presentations, a really clever mnemonic to help you with the first few minutes of any presentation to get it off to the right start and give you lots of confidence to continue.

*   A – Attention
*   B – Benefits
*   C – Credibility
*   D - Direction

Attention

"Unaccustomed as I am to public speaking…."

"Hello, my name is Paul Archer…"

"Um, okay, let's get started then, shall we?"

What do these three have in common? Yes, of course, they are bland, listless, and terribly unexciting presentation starters.

Your first priority is to get the attention of your audience, especially if you are selling and presenting at the same time. We don't have the luxury of time, so we need to grab their attention in the first few moments.

Now it helps if you've done your circulating with the audience beforehand and have done some homework on the people sitting in front of you. This gives you some pointers as to the type of attention getter to use.

I'm not saying you should tell a joke. Perhaps you could but make sure it's a self-effacing joke to show your humility and not embarrass anyone sitting down.

- Share a quotation. You can get thousands of these from the Internet, and one might fit the bill.

- Tell a story or metaphor which will link into the main points.

- Ask a searching question.

- A call to action

- This day in history. Log onto the History Channel's website and sign up for the email-a-day service. It's great, and every day gives you something that happened this day in history. You might be able to link this in.

Benefits

Once you have their attention, tease them with some of the main benefits or the major one benefit they will get from listening to maybe start taking action.

It might be obvious to you, but we have to think of our audience. WIIFM. What's in it for me? Think in their shoes and share some benefits.

"What I'd like to do is to give you some bang up-to-date pointers which will help you decide your direction over the next year. These could give you a competitive advantage."

Enough to intrigue, excite, and make people want to listen more.

Credibility

Important to get this part done, if the audience has never met you before. Sometimes, in more formal settings, the master of ceremonies will introduce you and help to build your credibility.

However, in most business presentations, particularly sales pitches or "beauty parades", you really do have to cement your credibility. Don't overdo this bit. Don't fall into the trap of telling them all about you, your history, your qualifications.

That's zzzzz time.

Instead use a reassurance statement. This statement should include your name and your experience both in the customer's industry or sector and your experience in dealing with similar problems to your customer.

"My name is Paul Archer. I've been working with salespeople across the globe for almost twenty years helping them to earn their bonuses. For the last two years I've been helping businesses like yours get better closing ratios from their key accounts."

Direction

I love taking my three children on car journeys. My wife and I have a bet as to when the first one will ask, "Are we there yet, Dad?" Normally my wife wins. So I reply, "Not yet Euan. We've just passed Winchester, and we'll probably be at Nanas in half an hour."

And they're happy for the next few miles.

Now someone gave me a brilliant tip the other week to help in this arduous purpose. Keep telling them where you are and how long to go.

"Hey, guys, we've just passed Stonehenge. Can you see it on your right? And we'll be at Nanas in twenty minutes, in time for an ice cream"

Since that piece of advice, we've never looked back and you can use the same idea in your presentations.

Tell your audience where you're going to take them. Give them clear direction. Not an agenda. These are for books. Presentations need signposts which tell you where you're going. At each junction the audience needs reminding where they've come from and then where they're going to go next.

The best analogy is one of these property purchase programmes on the TV. My favourite is Phil and Kirsty doing *Location, Location, Location*. Just as they're coming up to a commercial break, Kirsty will quickly recap the main points covered so far and one or two tempters of what you'll see after the break. This not only gives you clear direction, but tempts you to come back after the break.

And when you return from the break, Phil takes over and reminds you what they did before the break and then tempts you further with the major benefits of the next fifteen minutes.

Brilliant stuff and certainly worth repeating in your presentations.

So give direction and then constantly signpost your way to the end. And as you approach the end signal that the end is in sight, summarise each of your key points. Remember the power of three – three major points maximum. Invite questions; never ever finish on a Q&A because if there are no questions, you'll go out like a damp squid.

And now you know your ABC…and D. Next time will you sing with me…

The drake and motivation

At the last count we have twelve chickens including one cockerel, and earlier this year we inherited a duck, just one, and he's a drake. We have a number of coops, and they all mixed well together, laying eggs for my breakfast.

But there was something wrong. The drake seemed subdued, solemn. He was not happy so my wife popped over to a local farmer and bought four female ducks and introduced them to the flock.

We'd found our drake's hot button, his WIIFM, so I took a photograph.

Notice how proud he is, his head held high, scampering around with excitement, and closely followed by his badelynge of girls, who adore him.

We found what intrinsically gave him motivation.

You see, you can't motivate people, salespeople, or anyone, in fact. You can only provide them with something, or surround them with something, and they motivate themselves from within.

We know this, don't we?

My message is to find out what it is that will help your people to motivate themselves, explore their hot buttons, their WIIFMs, and provide it to them, if you can.

90

Our drake is a different duck now since we provided him with his WIIFM, and the eggs the ducks lay are to die for. Larger than hen eggs, with a glorious orange yolk. I have a surplus each day so if anyone is passing, just text me and you can savour them yourselves.

A different way of doing course introductions...

...without being corny.

Course introductions are really important to set the scene for learning, especially if the group have never met each other before, but they can be time-consuming, and the usual going around the room actually puts the fear into more people than you think.

Here's a suggestion to make it slightly easier for them to talk, yet keep the topic light and to encourage some humour. We all know that these ingredients will relax people and set the scene.

Have printed on cards, the following questions:

1. I've always wondered about...
2. If I could stay at any age, I'd like to be...
3. If I had the day off tomorrow, I would...
4. The most fun thing I did this year is...
5. I've always wanted to (but never had the courage to)....

Ask everyone to prepare their answers to the questions. Depending on the size of your group you could:

- Put them into pairs to ask each other or coach each other the questions. (This is a good starter when conducting coaching workshops.)

- Put them into small teams, maybe the people on each table, to think about their answers and discuss them amongst the group.

- Have people present their answers at the front, using the cards as prompts (useful if you're doing presentation skills or train the trainer).

But I'm sure you've already thought of another way to use this exercise.

How to focus on your audience

Are you a PowerPoint Gazer?

In the early 1990s a music genre began called shoe gazers, and as you've guessed, the guitarists would play whilst staring at their shoes. They looked odd, but the music they produced was terrific.

Shoe gazers launched the success of many Britpop and indie bands. One of my favourites was Elastica.

Enough of the music reminiscing.

Whiz forward in time and we have a new genre, but not in music, but for business presenters called PowerPoint gazers – presenters who constantly gaze at their PowerPoint slides because these remind them of what to talk about. They don't know their material well enough or haven't taken steps to prepare their content.

This makes them too content-focussed as they spend brain power thinking and remembering what to say. It takes their attention away from their audience.

Dangerous.

I know why; so do you. Because we're busy and can't find the time to prepare. However, we need to master our content if we're to honour our audience – if we don't, we're not caring for our paid audience. Remember, audiences pay with their precious time, not just money.

Allow me to offer you some tips and strategies which I've gleaned after professionally presenting for over twenty years.

I'm going to start with how you can create prompts and notes, then how to practice and memorise your speech, and finally, on the day of the presentation, how to keep on track with your content.

All allowing you to focus exclusively on your audience and not become a PowerPoint Gazer.

Prompts and notes

Glance'able notes

My first training team weaned in the early 1990s, as shoe gazers became of age and were all successful salespeople who I plucked from the field sales force to become excellent trainers. Our challenge was to help them stay audience focussed whilst presenting top-drawer content. I began by teaching them how to make notes that they could refer to during the sessions to keep on track and remember the key points required. For Christmas, I bought them plastic recipe book stands to house their notes with one aim.

So they could glance at the notes during their session without taking their eyes off their most precious resource – the audience – but still know what to talk about.

And I recommended three varieties of notes – mind maps, bullets on card, and the A4 sheets that PowerPoint produces for notes. All these were placed on the recipe stand.

Mind Maps

I'm sure you've come across mind maps before and maybe you create them regularly. I do for a variety of purposes, and one is notes whilst I'm running talks and presentations. Here's an example of a one-day seminar.

This stays at the front of my presentation on my recipe book stand to enable me to glance and remember the section I was talking about. Maybe you could create these to remind you of what to say. I like to use colour and pictures to help me remember parts of my trainings and talks. The trick is to glance at the notes when needed, not to stop and read them halfway through – that's amateurish.

Bullets

Bullets are summarised points, i.e., a short one or two words describing the content of your talk. A series of bullets can summarise a whole one-hour talk or a seven-hour seminar. Each bulleted word should spark your brain to recall a series of information, points, stories to enable you to present that area of your talk. That's all that is needed if you have put your time into preparing the content.

Your bullets can look as you like them to look, but they must be glance'able from a distance of three feet or one metre so make the font size large enough to see at a distance.

PowerPoint notes

PowerPoint provides its own note page; you may have seen it. It helps you to print out the slides with your own notes underneath the slide. These work so long as you keep the notes you make brief enough and large to be able to read them using the three-foot rule.

The major problem with this method is you end up with a collection of sheets of paper which can look clumsy and awkward when presenting. I've seen speakers use these when presenting from the dreaded podium, and very few use them well as they have a tendency to type lots of notes and practically read these to the audience. Lack of preparation.

They are useful for preparing and practising your talk though.

Political speakers and heads are trained to read these in their presentations, but they are weaned off reading as such and trained to capture a sentence or two by looking down. They then look up to engage the audience or camera and say their words. They repeat this process all the way through.

Practice before the event

I don't need to tell you that the more practice you do, the better your presentation. It relieves nerves, makes you more audience-centred, allows you to ad lib on the day, and come over more polished and professional.

The problem is time, or lack of it, especially if you work in a corporate environment.

My advice is to use your down time to practice. Create your talk first and transfer it to notes, cards, or mind maps – something to remind you. Make sure you're comfortable with the content and can carry your notes with you. Then you use down time to read out your talk and glance at your notes to remind you. Carry a master copy of the speech or slides.

But if it provides solace for you, many speakers miss out on large chunks of the content and the audience still gets the message.

Read out loud your speech in:

- The car
- Whilst walking the dog
- Out running
- In the shower (but don't take your notes in with you. The shower is the best place to memorise the first five minutes of your talk. Yes, you need to do this.
- On the plane (but read to yourself)
- In the gym
- Waiting for the kids at the school gates
- Whilst cooking the dinner
- Doing the housework

The list goes on.

Future pacing the talk

Once you've nailed the talk, consider future pacing your presentation. This is a splendid way of relieving nerves and creating bucket loads of confidence. It firms up your timings as well and allows you to immediately connect with your audience when you arrive because you've practiced.

I've been known to future pace my entire presentation of forty-five minutes by visualising where I am, the audience reactions, the use of slides, my interactive exercises, and questions from the audience, particularly the Q&A.

It's what I do for a living so I make the time, but I do appreciate that some of you reading this may not be able to find this precious resource, so try speed rehearsal instead.

Speed rehearsal

Speed rehearsal is used by actors to rehearse and practice their script and scene. In their heads or out loud they just talk through their lines as quickly as they can. So a forty-five-minute talk might take you nineteen minutes with speed rehearsal, but it has a positive effect on you recalling what to say on the day.

Leverage your preparation

I like leveraging – it's my goal for the next few years. I try to eke out some other benefit when performing talks. An example is my downtime when I'm preparing for a talk. Whilst practising or reading out the talk, have you thought about recording it to MP3 using your laptop, tablet, or smartphone?

You can achieve a reasonable quality using the latest technology and don't need to splash out sums on microphones and software.

The MP3 can be used for a variety of purposes. Add it to your blog for downloading, and send a link to the audience after the talk as a way to reinforce their learning. Generation Y will love this as they were born with earphones grafted to their heads.

And of course, you can use it to help you remember the talk by playing it to yourself during your downtime. People have been known to go to sleep listening to the talk and swear that subliminally they remember every word. Clever, but I roll over and hurt my ears during my sleep so I've never mastered this.

Memorise your talk through a journey

Do you ever travel the same journey time after time? A journey or a route which you know like the back of your hand, a short journey around your garden, through your house, a car route, a train trip.

If so, you're well on the way to memorising your talk effortlessly and presenting with no cards or prompts at all. Let me show you how.

First you need to put your talk onto index cards or A4 sheets, and this must be represented by key points, bullets of one or two words. Make sure the talk hangs together and you're not going to change it anymore.

Now for each bullet that you've written, I want you to visually create something to represent the bullet. Something totally weird and visual; a three-dimensional object is best. For example, your bullet might say USA comparison. So you put a picture of the Statue of Liberty in your head but elaborate this image by putting a big, beaming smile on her face because the comparison figures you want to show the audience are very positive numbers.

Or you might have "Financial Services Authority" as a bullet point, so you create a picture of Canary Wharf in London with little grey men with bowler hats emerging one-by-one looking very sombre and officious.

Now the fun part begins. Start your route in your head, and at every major point in the journey place your object firmly so you can see it clearly. Put them in the right order of your speech.

Next run through your journey in your head and visualise every image you've created. There's nothing to stop you physically going on the journey and seeing the item. I often do this when I'm using the garden or the house as my route, but for longer journeys I use my imagination.

I've been known to place up to thirty-five items in my journey – each item represents a bullet point, a part of my talk, and because of the power of visual memory, I've been able to recall every single image. Try it, it works.

On the day

The slurp technique

This one never fails, even in large conference rooms when you're presenting to hundreds of people. To drink water in the middle of your talk is as acceptable as breathing, so combine your drink with a quick glance at your notes placed carefully next to your bottle or glass of water.

It's that simple; I do it every time even if I never glance at my notes. Sometimes just having your notes on hand is enough to calm your nerves.

Note placement

Your notes can be surreptitiously placed around your presentation arena. I've been known to stick my notes to the back of a flip chart, on the floor if I'm on a stage as the audience can't see them, on Post-it notes on the wall when training, next to my PowerPoint remote control, at the back of the room on a poster.

Slide jogger

One of the most frustrating aspects of a talk is forgetting which slides are coming next when you have a mainly slide-based presentation. For those of us who can't find the time, we create slides to help us remember. You know my views here. However, slides do have their place in effective presentations. A tip here is to print out a handout version of your slides with nine on each page, number them, and keep this close to your notes so you can glance at the next slide before you reveal.

That way you can correctly alert the audience to the next slide rather than clicking on the next slide, glancing at it to remind you of what to say.

Dropbox

In case you lose your notes, ensure you've scanned or photographed them and download them to a service such as Dropbox.

Copy the public link to your smartphone so you can quickly download them from a convenient hotel PC and print them off before your presentation starts. Plan B's are well recommended.

Next steps

The trend of shoe gazing came to an abrupt end as the audience fought back. The band members just weren't engaging with their fans, so the practice had to stop.

Likewise try and prevent the onset of PowerPoint gazing by planning, practicing, and reminding yourself of your talk so you can free up your attention and concentration, thus ensuring your audience has an experience to remember.

Always have a Plan B

I often travel abroad via Heathrow Airport. On my return, I have a number of public transport options – train, coach, Express. I've tried them all, and I used to make a fatal stress-inducing mistake.

Let me explain.

I would calculate the return of the airplane and approximate time through passport control and luggage collection, and then pre-book a train ticket or coach ticket to get me home.

Every time I came home, I would stress out as I was on a deadline, and if the plane was delayed or held in a big queue in the sky, or there was a hold-up in passport control, I would literally sweat anxiety because I was going to miss my train or bus.

Now I have a plan B. I book flexible tickets for an expected arrival time but make a note of the future buses and trains that I can catch if I'm delayed, which I always am. This morning I was delayed a total of three hours flying British Airways from Dubai. But I had my contingency rail air coach and train from Reading.

Simple really, and we all know this. But what about in your role as a trainer? Do you have adequate Plan B's. Do you:

- Take copies of your running notes and put them into a public place in Dropbox and make a note of the link on your smartphone.

- Likewise do you do the same with your PowerPoint or Prezi slides?

- Do you have your media on a USB stick in case your laptop gets stolen or broken?

- Your handouts, do you keep a master copy of each one on your person in the hotel room, just in case your car, with all the handouts, is stolen during the night? Plus a master copy in your Dropbox public folder?

- At the location of your training, do you ensure you get in early and work out fire procedures, lunches, etc.?

- If the technology fails, are you able to resume without it, a back-up plan, maybe extra flip chart paper?

- If people are late, say there's been terrible congestion, do you have a way of shortening your programme without losing the impact? Can you do the same at the end without losing the effect?

- Do you have someone who can step in your shoes if you're taken ill suddenly? A locum?

- If you're online delivering, do you have a plan B for a technical shutdown?

- If you lose the WiFi, do you have a wireless dongle you can plug into your laptop or PC so you can continue?

- If your webcam breaks down, do you have a spare or a laptop or tablet with one built in?

- If you're doing video on your programme, do you have a backup camera, maybe a small one in the case operating from an SD card or a small tripod which you can use to rig up your iPhone to video record?

Maybe a little paranoid there, Mr Archer, but clients pay me for an experience which is consistent and brings results. Problems do happen to delay or wreck plans.

Just ask British Airways, who have ruined my Sunday which I was hoping to spend with my family from midday onwards, but I won't be getting home until after dark now. I did tweet it, so maybe I might get something in return to sweeten the pill.

Straight to Google – how to use your Learner's Smartphones

Last week I was doing the microphone voiceovers for a large conference and was being helped out by an eighteen-year-old lad. Smashing guy he was, and we enjoyed the odd moments of conversation about this, that, and the other.

I spotted a trend surfacing when conversing with Nathan. Every now and then, when our conversation took a turn and we needed to clarify something, or confirm a fact or a statement, he went straight to Google.

Straight to Google on his smartphone.

Now this isn't unusual or indeed difficult to do, with the simplicity of smartphones nowadays and always on Internet, but what struck me was he regarded it as the norm when having a conversation. Generation Y's think more about their next power up for their smartphones than their next meal. Their smartphone is a third limb, a second brain, an essential organ.

And this got me thinking about training and speaking in public where for years we've encouraged our audiences to switch off and stop checking email.

I think this is a dated approach. Instead use them to the workshop or talk's advantage. Here're some ideas to add to yours:

1. When doing role play, you could create a telephone-based scenario and get them to role play this using their smartphones. All you need to do is ask them to write their mobile numbers on the white board and pair them off.

2. Use an SMS polling software whereby they can use their phones to enter a poll and have the results displayed up on the big screen. I use http://www.smspoll.net

3. Ask them to text you questions rather than asking in person. This works well for large groups when people might be intimidated to ask normally. Have the questions display on the big screen. Naturally you can put out a hashtag and get them to tweet instead, but not everyone tweets – believe me they don't – but most people text.

4. Every now and then ask the group to Google a fact or something. Ensure this comes over as part of your plan, not because you don't know the answer. Have a small prize for the person who comes up with the answer first.

5. Put up a brief quiz on the screen and let them Google the answers.

6. Have them phone their phones to leave a message the next time you're doing vocal training or presentation skills, so they can hear themselves.

7. Test their listening skills when on the phone by allowing them to phone a friend in the room and listen. You can even have the call recorded and pinged to their email inbox as a sound file for listening later. Email me if you want to know how.

8. Use the audio and video record functions of their phones by asking groups to create a mini movie. It could be to summarise some of their key learnings from the day or to illustrate a topic from the course schedule. Have them create the video and ask them to upload to a video channel you've just created on YouTube or to their own channel. Fire up YouTube on your laptop and view.

There are a few ideas. I'm sure they've inspired you to come up with some better ones. Use the phones rather than subdue them. Gone are those days when people will diligently switch off their Blackberries – get with the twenty-first century.

How to banish boring beginnings

If you're like me, a little jaded with our usual starts, then this idea will inspire you. Do you find introducing yourself and running through the objectives of the session on PowerPoint rather dull and uninspiring? Then join the club. Many trainers do, and our groups find them even more tedious than we do.

So what's the answer?

So long as the objectives, agenda, etc. have been emailed to them beforehand to satisfy the detailed hungry ones, then simply tell a story.

Craft a story that introduces the objectives and intention of your session and shouts about you as well. Here's one I prepared earlier.

"They were halfway through their induction training for the Prudential Insurance Company where I worked as a corporate trainer, and I was training on the subject of pensions. A recipe for snooze time if you're not careful.

It was spring 1991. The World Wide Web was only two years old and the first Gulf War had just finished. My training room was dim and warm. And my overhead projector box was heating up nicely, displaying my wordy visuals against the screen. In those days, PowerPoint for Windows had only just been coded and visuals weren't even heard of. No, it was words only on the screen.

I was just twenty-eight. I'd been selling all my life and had just been promoted into training, and I felt so proud. As a brand new training officer, my job was to teach them all about pensions and to inspire them to learn.

Did I succeed?

Did I, heck. I remember the moment. As morning turned into afternoon, this one chap who had been sniffing the flip chart pens all morning was beginning to nod off, as was the person next to him. I suppose the best news was that I spotted it before their heads crashed to the table, so I called a break immediately.

I'd goofed. I'd committed the primal sin of all trainers. I'd fashioned every ingredient that meant snooze time—the room, the content, the warmth, toxic flip chart pens, the whirring old overhead projector. And the cake was baked and they fell asleep.

I was so embarrassed, I swore I'd never do that again and began my odyssey of learning how to train properly. Not by watching the other trainers in the company. Most were the same as me at that moment. A couple of people were the exception, and I made a goal to learn how to train adults in a way that ensured I kept their attention and that they enjoyed themselves, used all their senses, and remained in a state of positive learning all day.

And that's exactly what we're going to do today. My name is Paul Archer, and yes, I was that young trainer way back in 1991. Since that day I've learnt all the strategies and techniques to modernise my training workshops, and I'm going to share with you everything I've learnt over the past twenty-five years."

Now that story:

- Tells the group about me and that I've been training for over twenty years. Some people need to know this, but I don't like to brag.

- If my audience are in financial services, it builds a rapport because so am I.

- It points out a problem they might have faced at some time.

- It subtly knocks PowerPoint word-only slides.

- It tells them quite clearly what we are aiming to do today, in other words banish boring training.

- It has humour so displays my training style.

- It is self-effacing and shows a goof on my part, and this builds rapport.

All done on a subconscious level so the messages filter in without boring them.

Practice your story, and you should type it out and memorise it. Don't rely on winging it. Professionals don't wing it; they rehearse. And then tell your story and it will be the same time after time. Stories have this sequence…set the scene, introduce the character, the journey, the obstacle, overcoming the obstacle (I goofed, remember), and the learning.

So my call to action is to think of a story from your life that not only introduces you, but also illustrates the objectives of the session. This will ensure you banish boring beginnings.

The Steven Spielberg start

Have you ever had the course feedback along the lines of "slow to start" or "could have got going a bit quicker"? I'm sure they haven't been as blunt as those, but occasionally we might feel that our starts are a little slow since we have to cram so much in. Our introduction, their introduction, fire escape procedures, agendas…the list goes on.

Try the Steven Spielberg start next time to add variety and interest. This very famous movie director would often start his films with an intense action sequence or clip that immediately gained your attention, then the titles would follow.

Many movies do the same. James Bond is another example.

Think how you can do this on your courses. Here are some examples of starts I've used in the past.

- Mobile phone activity to kick things off.
- A group exercise from minute one, where I asked teams to head to the four corners of the room, reveal the flip sheet waiting for them, and to tackle the question in two minutes and prepare a presentation.
- A good, engaging and connected story.
- A SQUARE-based question session.
- An engaging video clip, I mean really fetching.

I'm sure you can think of activities that you can bring forward from your workshop and make these your Steven Spielberg starts.

The One-Breath Introduction

Last week, I ran a number of three-hour workshops for a dozen or so people.

Nothing wrong in that, of course, except a tight time frame.

Tight enough for us to dispense with group introductions, and that's dangerous. If the group doesn't know each other or they're fearful of anyone in the workshop, then they're simply not going to open up, discuss, or cooperate with you.

So here's a great way to do short and punchy introductions. It's called the one-breath introduction.

Explain to the group that we have plenty to cover today, and you'd like some brief introductions from each person on the call so we're going to do the one-breath introduction.

Further explain that they can breathe in, and whilst they breathe out, they can tell you:

1. Why they are here
2. What they do
3. Their favourite stretch of water

Or whatever you want them to say in their introduction, but they must do it with one breath.

It's a really cool introduction technique, is quite fun, and gets the point across that you want to quickly get down to work.

P.S. If you want to find out what the stretch of water tells you about someone, email me. It's too racy for a blog post or email.

The Body Language of Public Speaking

Next time you watch a politician on TV speaking to an audience, turn the volume down and watch. Then interpret what is being said just by observing the body language. Try it – it's amazing what you read into the message just by watching the person speaking.

How many of you have made your mind up about a speaker's message without concerning yourself about the words, rather, purely by observation and your intuition? And this is going on right now somewhere in the world. A business speaker has a good message but it's being clouded by the way it's presented.

The purpose of this section is to remind you—no, convince you of some key steps to take to ensure your body doesn't cloud the message next time you get up and speak.

Let's kick off with the body language and work around the body, reminding ourselves of what to do. We'll then cover movement around your stage.

The Head

My daughter has just started playgroup, and she brought home a picture of Daddy, an amazing picture showing Daddy with a large, smiling face and two arms and legs. However, the body was missing. This happened with my sons when they first went to playgroup.

DADDY
18TH Feb 2005

Inquisitive as ever, I asked the nursery teacher why Bethan had missed out the body. "Children of that age don't focus on the body. They are only concerned with the face and that's all they see. That's why clowns paint their faces so brightly and children love them."

As adults, we still have childish habits, and one of them is to focus on the face of someone who is speaking to you. So get those expressions working for you and really exaggerate the meaning. Smile, frown, look angry, shocked, amazed – but please always be congruent with your message.

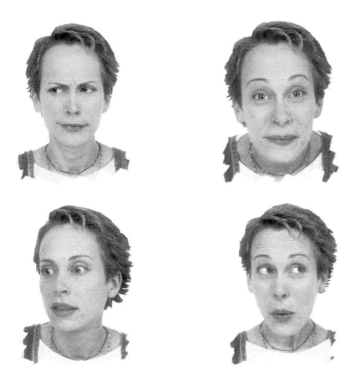

Eye Contact

Next we have eye contact. This is probably the one skill that, when mastered, does the most to engage the audience and build trust and rapport with the audience. The rule is to hardly ever let go. Imagine you're playing tennis or squash. You never let your eye off the ball, otherwise you'll miss a shot. Likewise, keep your eye contact on the audience at all times.

Careful with the lighthouse technique as well – this is where speakers sweep the audience in a repetitive swishing motion that does more to put people to sleep than engage.

It always reminds me of those old Second World War POW escape movies when the escapees are nudging their way out of the tunnel dodging the sweeping searchlights. As soon as the light has moved along its repetitive motion, they dash to safety. In a similar way your audience will escape you when your sweeping leaves them.

Instead have a conversation with your audience with your eyes. Randomly contact with each audience member and give them two to three seconds of eye contact before moving on to the next person. Maintain this random movement. Find those in the audience who like just a little more eye contact and be aware of those who want slightly less.

When faced with a large audience – I mean more than twenty-five or so people, adopt a similar habit, but don't give each person eye contact. That'll take ages. Instead clump people into small groups and give these clumps the same eye contact as if they were one person. I tell you, that because of the distance between you and a large audience, this gives people the impression that you are looking at them.

Feet

Now let's go to the other extreme of your body, your feet and legs. Now what do you do with these limbs? Not a lot really unless you are moving around your stage. That's movement with a purpose, not aimless wandering that only distracts the audience.

Do you remember your mother asking you to stand up straight? Maybe, and it really was good advice. Try to stand with both feet firmly on the ground pretty much the same distance apart as your shoulders. Keep them balanced so your body is not leaning to one side. Don't look like a catwalk model or like you're supping a pint at the bar of your local. Stand straight and look professional, not like a slouch.

Nerves…that's a word than conjures up fear and dread every time people stand up and speak in public. And sure enough, you'll have nerves. Professionals call it adrenaline, and you need that to do a really good job. If you don't have nerves or adrenaline, you might as well not bother because you can't be bothered. Sop welcome nerves, call them adrenaline, and make them work for you.

Nerves will show in the periphery of your body. The ends such as feet, hands, head. Keeping your feet still transfers this energy to the top part of your body where it should go.

Now I didn't say you should stay rigid to the spot; that would be terrible for twenty minutes. Instead focus your attention on preventing aimless movement, pacing up and down, shifting from side to side. Keep well-balanced and professional.

The Body

Next we have the trunk. That's the bit my daughter missed out. Not much you can do with the trunk apart from keeping it straight. Not like the sergeant major on the parade ground but not slouched either—rather, relaxed and comfortable. The worst sin is to block the invisible mid line that runs from between your two feet and your head. Block it and you place a barrier with your audience. Just don't block it – that's the rule.

Hands and Arms

Next the arms and hands. I've spoken with hundreds of people who honestly don't know what to do with their hands.

Shame really, so they copy people on the TV, especially weather girls. They grasp their hands together. I've never understood this although I was guilty myself once. It made me feel better and comfortable so much that as soon as I stood up to talk, my two hands came together. And when I got really nervous, I used to rub them together too. Someone told me I looked like a market trader making lots of money. That sure went down well with my audiences.

So what do you do with them? Behind your backs, but that just reminds me of Prince Charles. In your pockets I hear you say. No, you're hiding something, keeping back from the audience, and besides, you're missing out on a great weapon. No, the answer is to use them to back up your message by gesturing.

I did some training work in the Netherlands earlier this year for an international food company. The delegates were from all over Europe – Spain, Italy, Germany, Netherlands, France…I watched each one present on many occasions, and it was so great to watch those from Mediterranean countries who naturally speak with their hands. They gesture so well, and when given the go-ahead to gesture during their speeches, they really went for it. Us Anglo Saxons are the stilted ones and need to learn to speak with our hands.

A decade ago I hit age forty. One of my dying wishes was to go to Glastonbury, and that year I finally bought the tickets. I hired a camper van for the weekend; I still like some creature comforts. When I watched the bands playing on the Pyramid stage, I was so far away I could barely see the singer. And the lead singer knows this so his gestures were dramatic. If he wanted us to clap, he wouldn't politely pat his hands together; he launched them over his head to make a very dramatic clap.

This is how we should gesture with audiences. Large, dramatic gestures to help the audience understand what you're saying. Broad gestures that welcome every person into your speech, building rapport. Think of your speech content and let your hands do the talking. Watch deaf people doing their sign language – it really is a very clever way of finding your gesture buttons.

And when not gesturing or talking, maybe standing still to take questions from your audience, assume the assertive stance. Standing straight with your arms and hands down your sides in a relaxed, assertive, and confident manner.

Body Movement

Finally, body movement. Movement can be an enormously effective way of engaging the audience into your message. Clean your stage – remove obstacles, tape wires to the floor, so you don't trip over them. Place the screen to the side.

Yes, to the side, and I wish more meeting planners would situate their screen to the right or left of the audience and not bang in the middle. You've probably been there or seen it. The slides are beaming onto the screen. The table is full of people, so to let the person on your left see the screen, you move into the corner of the room. You're lost, you're gone – you've lost eye contact with the audience who are busy reading the slides.

If you're able to position the screen to the left or right of the audience, you'll be able to remain in the centre of the stage. Trust what is on your slides and be aware of reading directly from the screen – this takes your eye contact away from the audience and is a cardinal sin. Have a laptop screen in front of you or learn your slides. Better still, use fewer of them, but that's another story.

Once you have a clear space, do move around with a purpose. I've used past, present, and future by gradually moving along an imaginary line. The audience can see the time moving along as well as hear. I've used one side of the stage, being advantages of an idea I'm promoting, and the other side, the disadvantages. I've placed flip charts at both sides of the room to mirror these place anchors.

Move forward towards your audience when you want to make a really big point. Move backwards when you want them to reflect on something. Move to your left or right to change the subject or pace of your delivery.

Do move around your stage but with a distinct purpose.

The next time you're observing and listening to a speaker, try and cut out the sound and focus entirely on the visual aspects. Try and interpret what he or she is saying just by the body language alone. You may not be right in your assumption of the meaning, but it's the impression that everyone else is probably getting too. And first impressions last for ages.

Training with SQuARE eyes

I remember the moment well. I'd been taught SQuARE on a course and was so impressed I wanted to train everyone in my training team as soon as possible. I was taken aback by how easily a "chalk and talk" session could be turned from a one-way dialogue to an interactive session where delegates were challenged, excited, and rewarded.

You see, on a training course there are essentially two types of questions a trainer will ask— the testing question and the teaching question. Testing questions just test to see if the person has learnt or remembered what you're teaching them. They have their place but not all the time. Now teaching questions are a different kettle of fish altogether.

A teaching question literally teaches a subject to a group of people by asking them questions. Using SQuARE allows you to do this effortlessly and elegantly.

SQuARE is an acronym which stands for:

- Statement

- Question

- u answer

- Acknowledge

- Reward
- Explain

And you can SQuARE a training session from start to finish. Let me explain how to SQuARE.

Statement

We're looking to explain something to our group so we need to set some context or begin the subject we want to talk about. We make a statement about the subject. For example, let's say we wanted to teach people how to overcome an objection in selling. We could say something like:

"In selling, some customers like to voice concerns about the product we're selling."

Easy that one. Now let's go onto the question.

Question

Here we ask a short, open question with good tonality such as:

"From your experience, at what point in the sales cycle do most concerns get voiced?"

u answer

They answer. Once you've asked the question, PPP works well – pose, pause, pounce. Look around the group, encouraging an answer. Bob answers:

"Usually at the end when I ask them for the business."

Acknowledge

Thank the person for answering.

"That's great, thank you, Bob."

Reward

These last two often go together.

"That's great, thank you, Bob. You're spot on with many other salespeople."

Explain

This is your chance, as the trainer, to explain further Bob's answer to enable you to progress your explanation of the whole topic.

"Many salespeople experience customer concerns at the end of the sales process, and this is really frustrating, don't you think? The fact of the matter is, that we then spend time trying to overcome these, and it can sometimes put off the customer buying the product."

Next you swing back around to the beginning again. Back to the statement.

"It's a plain fact that handling concerns at the end of the sales process is not ideal."

Next, the question.

"What sort of problems can this cause salespeople?"

Now you've started the process again. Someone will answer and you can acknowledge and reward and explain again. Someone says it makes them dread the close and may put them off actually closing, so your explanation might be along the lines of:

"I can understand how you feel there. If I knew the customer was going to object after I'd close, I think human nature would be to not close. And that's no good when we're selling."

Back to the statement.

"So there're many problems handling concerns at the end of the sales interview. Let's say we moved this handling to the beginning or heart of the selling interview and handled them then. What difference would this make to you?"

Having received various answers and acknowledged, rewarded, and explained, you can then swing back around to the statement again.

"So it appears that the benefits are stacked up for earlier handling of objections. One method is to pre-empt the objection before it even is mentioned by the customer. In other words, handle it before it becomes an issue."

On to the question.

"Taking your product, what are the typical client concerns that always cause people trouble?"

And then you can ask questions around how best to pre-empt these.

Do you see where we're going with SQuARE? We're not using the "guess what's coming up question", which is easy to answer. We're trying to make our group think. The answers aren't obvious, and the trainer is steering the session and guiding the delegates. We're making them work and at the same time getting them involved in the explanation process, which is so very typically a one-way street – trainer to delegate.

And that's what modern training is all about – involvement. It's the one advantage that face-to-face training has over other means of delivery, such as Internet-based, CD-based, DVDs, MP3s.

These struggle to truly involve delegates, but face-to-face learning has to involve, otherwise there's no point doing it this way as the other methods are far cheaper to administer in the long run.

The Golden Rules of the Q&A

Do you ever have to deliver presentations and include a question-and-answer session? Read on to discover the golden rules to make this part of your talk shine.

I was at a conference recently, and the speaker, who had done a pretty good job with his presentation, was about to take questions from the fifty-plus audience.

It was time for the dreaded Q&A session. And you could tell this speaker wasn't looking forward to it as his body language closed down and his voice demonstrated fear and trepidation.

As always, audiences want speakers to do well. It's a human DNA thing. No one wants a speaker to bomb. And I was hoping this speaker would follow the golden rules of Q&A's and do a good job.

Let me remind you of the golden rules.

Question-and-answer sessions are excellent audience participation techniques that work really well with larger groups where spontaneous questions just don't work. I mean for groups of twenty-plus. They allow the speaker to demonstrate their knowledge or wisdom. They encourage audience involvement, and they help the presentation to be linked to the needs and problems of the audience.

So you should run Q&A's.

But you simply mustn't leave them to the last moment. That's a recipe for a damp squid close. Ending on a Q&A can be risky because you don't know how many questions you're going to get, and it could all end rather meekly.

No, you should plan to run a Q&A session about two-thirds into the presentation, when content has been delivered and the audience inspired and educated.

If you must leave the Q&A to the end, plan a finish to your talk – your call to action or summary or "bang" as I call it – but have your Q&A before this planned close. That way, if you get few questions, then you just launch into your planned finish, to end on a high.

If you're worried about getting few questions, prime some audience members beforehand. Alternatively display your mobile number on the big screen and get people to text you questions as the presentation is delivered. This works very well for younger audiences where mobile phones are their third limb.

If you really want to be really clever, use an audience polling system using mobile phones. When this works it's very smart and ignites audiences who love to hear what others think. I use http://www.smspoll.net

When taking questions, follow this template:

- Repeat

- Respond

- Review

Hopefully you have a roving microphone, so everyone can hear the question. But it's always good practice to repeat the question to make sure everyone can hear it. There's nothing more frustrating than a question from the audience that others can't hear. You lose interest.

Repeating also gives you valuable thinking time whilst you formulate the answer in your head.

Respond, of course, although if the question is totally irrelevant, it's quite okay to park it and suggest you have a one-to-one later. You might upset the questioner but you'll please everyone else in the audience.

Respond quickly and succinctly. Don't ramble on and on. This is a game of tennis with both players involved in an exciting rally. Question, answer, next question, answer, next question, and so on.

Give the audience value by getting through a lot of questions if you can.

Finally review the answer. Ask the questioner, "Was that useful?" or "Has that helped you?" And then move on to the next question. A little tip here, if the questioner is hostile in any way – trying to catch you out or demonstrate their own expertise, which some do, then don't do the review. When you've answered the question, say something like "I think we have another question over here" and move on.

A final Q&A tip for you is to focus your eye contact on the whole audience with about 30% of your attention on the questioner. This helps to keep the audience engaged. It also prevents you getting tied in with continuous questions from one person, which is equally wearisome for the whole audience.

Keep to your timing that you allocated to the Q&A. Thank the audience for their questions and move on to the grand finale that you prepared.

And you've made the dreaded Q&A an integral part of your presentation.

My speaker from earlier. How did he do? He did okay, had excellent technical knowledge, which was evident from his presentation anyway. He repeated the question, which was good, but tended to ramble on with his answer. This is quite common from technical expert speakers, unfortunately. And he got a fair few questions. He did well and the audience was thrilled.

Tuning your listening to the next level

"Daddy, are you listening to me?" This sent me spluttering over my cornflakes and drizzling milk down my freshly ironed shirt. "I'm listening, Bethan, honest," knowing full well that I was merely looking at my daughter and hadn't followed a word she was saying.

Shame on you, Daddy.

"Sorry, Bethan, what did you say?"

"It doesn't matter now, Daddy."

Gone forever that conversation, and my daughter sulked for the rest of the breakfast, all because I simply hadn't listened. I got stuck in my own little world, relating everything to me and my concerns. Although I was carrying out classic active listening gestures – you know, eye contact, face tilt, nodding, those little "uh-uhs", I wasn't really listening.

But a woman is better skilled than us men at communicating – that's been proven time and time again. And my daughter, at only five, can spot when a man isn't listening properly.

Okay, I kind of got away with it this morning over breakfast...I think...I'll wait until tonight to see if Bethan is still talking to me. But in sales you won't get away with it. You'll lose the sale, and that's not so good. Imagine if your customer turned round to you and said, "You're not really listening to me, are you?"

That would be a killer, wouldn't it?

When practising rapport selling, not listening properly is practically a hanging offence. So how do we really do this? Two things.

1. One. Kick out active listening techniques. They don't work. They're false because just by giving the impression that you're listening doesn't add up. My daughter saw straight through me this morning, and your customer will too.

2. Two. Just know that listening is hard work and you have to concentrate on it. Someone once said to me many years ago that listening is really tough. At the time I thought this was nonsense and argued that talking was harder. How could I have been so wrong? You have to literally concentrate on listening to get it right.

And when you do, the rewards are immense in selling. You build a rapport quickly. You find out about your customer – their needs, wants, desires, criteria – their problems and concerns. You know when to give benefits; you know when there's a customer concern coming up; you know when to close. And these things make up selling.

So how do we do it? Think three levels of listening – a bit like a volume control on your iPod. When you want to listen more, just turn up your volume control. I know it sounds a little bit daft, but I have this imaginary volume control in my head, and when I'm selling or consulting with clients and I want to turn up my listening, I turn up my volume control and this tells my brain to start listening more.

My volume control has three levels – level 1, level 2, and level 3.

So let me tell you about these.

Level 1 listening

Level 1 listening, or internal listening, is when we are listening to sounds and information around us that are just for our purposes and no one else. I recall September 11th and having to use Edinburgh airport to fly home. Great timing on my part, eh? The airport was in chaos. There were security checks everywhere, people shouting and panicking – it was a nightmare.

There I was fully aware of what was going on and intent on getting home safely and on time. I was in level 1 listening mode and I didn't care about anyone else. I just wanted to hear the information and sounds that would mean that I got home. I listened for the broadcasts and particularly the word 'Birmingham'. I kept my ears open for information that would help me and no one else.

When people talk to you, do you relate what they are saying to your experience? When someone has told you they went skiing this year, did you immediately relate this to your last skiing holiday and talk about that? We've all done it, haven't we? Inadvertently we're level 1 listening and thinking only of ourselves.

At level 1 our attention is on ourselves. We listen to the words of the other person, but the focus is on what it means to us. At level 1 the spotlight is on me – my thoughts, my judgments, my feelings, my conclusions about myself and others.

Have you ever been thinking about what you are going to say next? We all do this.

So turn up your volume control now to level 2 and feel the difference.

Level 2 listening

Level 2 listening, or focused listening, comes next.

At level 2 there is a sharp focus on the other person. You can see it in people's posture when they are communicating at level 2. Probably both leaning forward, looking intently at each other. There is a great deal of attention on the other person and not much awareness of the outside world.

You are beginning to see their words and reasoning on their side of the fence. You've put yourself in their shoes and their world. The next time someone tells you about their holiday, relate their experiences to them—how they saw it, what they encountered, what feelings of excitement they had.

Your awareness is totally on the other person. You listen for their words, their expression, their emotion, everything they bring. You notice what they say, how they say it. You notice what they don't say. You see how they smile or hear the tears in their voice. You listen for what they value. You listen for their vision and what makes them energetic.

You switch off all distractions, and I know this can be difficult.

I remember one of my first sales jobs selling mortgages to clients of an estate agency in Guildford High Street. My desk was right bang in the front office by the door – not ideal. And if you want to see big windows, you only have to go as far as your nearest estate agents.

The distractions were enormous as we were on the main shopping street in town.

But you need to tune out all distractions and focus just on your client to be successful at level 2.

Now turn up your volume control to the maximum – level 3

Level 3 listening

Level 3 listening, or global listening, is the ultimate trainer's skill.

At level 3, you listen at 360 degrees. In fact, you listen as though you and the client were at the centre of the universe receiving information from everywhere at once. Level 3 includes everything you can observe with your senses: what you see, hear, smell, and feel – the tactile sensations as well as the atmosphere.

If level 2 is an old dial-up modem, level 3 is wireless broadband with no physical connections, just a room full of digital signals. We can't see these signals, but we know they're there. Level 3 uses these invisible signals.

My wife is great at level 3 listening – in fact, research suggests that women are better at this than men.

Some wonderful research was conducted by Allan and Barbara Pease and published in their book *Why Men Don't Listen and Women Can't Read Maps*.

For many people this is a new realm of listening. One of the benefits of learning to listen at level 3 is greater access to your intuition. From your intuition you receive information that is not directly observable, and you use that information just as you'd use words coming from the client's mouth. At level 3, intuition is simply more information.

Next time just try your level 3. Trust your intuition, your gut reaction, your sixth sense to hear what is not visibly there.

And next time I'm at the breakfast table stuck in my own little world listening to my daughter at level 1, I'll just have to turn up my imaginary volume control and listen to level 3 and see the difference in her beautiful blue sparkling eyes.

How to Brief a Group Exercise

Picture the scene. You're running a meeting and you've just set an exercise to be done in groups. After five minutes, they say to you, "What were we supposed to do?" or "How long have we got left?"

And you think to yourself, "I told them that five minutes ago."

Don't blame them, since the group's attention might have been somewhere else when you instructed them. They might have been worrying about working with other people, or they might have been thinking of what they were having for dinner, or just mulling over the last topic.

Here's a tip that'll make your life and theirs so much easier when it comes to setting up group exercises in your meetings.

After you've described the exercise, draw a large box on the flip chart and divide this into four small boxes. Head each box – activity, groups, timing, and feedback, and fill in the detail with the group.

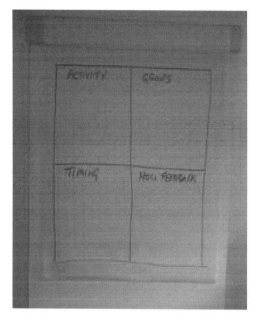

Activity is a brief synopsis of the activity. What are the groups you've agreed to? Timing should be the actual time the exercise should be finished by, not the duration of the exercise. Finally feedback should be how you wish each group to present their outcomes, if of course, you want them to.

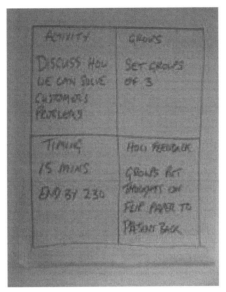

Leave the flip chart sheet showing for the group to refer to and you'll never have the problem again.

How to run the same workshop multiple times

Same old, same old – Better known as Soso.

This week I've been running a three-hour programme for different audiences. Nothing odd about that, but I've run the same programme sixteen times over the last two weeks.

I'm sure you've been there, too, and you end up forgetting what you said, and did you say that to that group, and did you tell that story before? It all gets very confusing.

So here are some tips to ensure each group gets a great experience.

• Use the same stories, but make sure they occur at exactly the same point in the programme. That way you'll not have the problem of thinking, "Did I tell this story to this group?"

• Break up the sessions; make them slightly different to add variety and interest to your delivery

• Re-order the sessions to enhance the programme – this is mainly for your sanity.

- Go for even more group involvement than normal, otherwise you'll tire quickly.

- Try not to make comparisons with previous groups – they want to know that they're unique and we're not comparing them to other groups.

- Deliberately put more energy into your delivery, voice, and mannerisms since you'll naturally slow down because you've delivered the same message time and time again.

- If there's someone in the room who was on a previous session, such as a manager, don't worry that they'll get the same delivery. Repeating a programme with the same first-class outcome is the sign of a true professional.

- Tell them at the end that they are the best group of all, and have a smirk on your face when you tell them.

Five Tips to Eliminate Nerves

Recently I was working with a number of managers to help them rid themselves of their nerves when speaking in business. It affects us all in differing ways. But what gives away your nerves when speaking?

Read on and I'll explain.

The cause of nerves

When we're nervous, the body pumps adrenaline into our system. This wonder drug is designed to give us strength to handle fighting or flighting. It increases our heart rate and pumps more blood around the system to enable us to perform the ancient ritual of defending ourselves or running away.

Unfortunately, when we're speaking in business situations we can neither fight the audience nor run away, but the body wants to.

The effects of adrenaline

So what does this do to us? A number of things. Some of us show this blood pressure buildup by the redness on our exposed skin. Mostly this can't be seen because of the distance, but the neck area is a dead giveaway, and this tends to be for women. You're best off hiding this if you can. I always enjoy my Professional Speaking Association events and I admire the female speakers. Many of them have fabulous scarves to cover their exposed neck areas. Even they have to hide what you can't prevent.

Men perspire more, especially under the armpits, and if you're wearing a dark shirt, this really shows the tell-tale mark of perspiration and nerves. Not good.

Simply wear a jacket if you know you will perspire, and don't remove it.

The butterflies

Blood flow around the tummy and intestines causes butterflies. You know that wobbly stomach-churning feeling when we get nervous?

The best strategy is to slow down your heart rate, and the easiest way is to breathe more and take full breaths. Try breathing through your diaphragm as this fills your lungs more and will slow your heart down to counteract the effect of adrenaline.

Fidgeting

Nerves make us all get fidgety, and our hands and feet can't stop moving. People pace up and down and side to side or just sway. Movement without a purpose is a dead giveaway that the presenter is nervous. Hands start to join together, and we fiddle with rings and grasp our knuckles.

The key here is to train ourselves to stand still and move our arms. Just like a tree, keep your trunk still and move your branches and leaves with the wind. Keep your feet still and move your upper half of your body. Expel all your energy and nerves through your arms and gestures. And don't link your hands together or hold onto anything as this will just exacerbate the problem.

Quivery voice

The voice changes when people get nervous. You start to hear a slight quiver like a radio station that's not quite tuned to the right channel. It just doesn't sound right. Your mouth becomes dry and you find it difficult to pronounce your words and you speed up as a natural result of the adrenaline.

Easy to solve. Drink lots of water beforehand. Keep off the coffee, coke, tea, and milk-based products such as cheese, mayonnaise. Have water with you when you present to business groups as this is so totally acceptable these days. Keep your prompt notes with your water so you can have a quick slurp and check your notes at the same time.

Train yourself to speak slower to prevent the speedy talking when nervous. Put more pause in between to create a similar effect.

And most importantly, don't wing it. Plan and prepare thoroughly…practice, practice, practice.

One-to-One Training

Medic

Occasionally you stumble across something really clever that you find yourself using time and time again. Early in my career, I came across MEDIC, a really simple but ever-so-clever acronym that just makes every training session you ever deliver bring results.

MEDIC can be used when you're putting together a session with only a few minutes' preparation so it's great with one-to-one training or "Sitting with Nellie"-type training.

Use the system and your sessions will work and be well-structured. MEDIC is an acronym which stands for:

• Motivate

• Explain

• Demonstrate

• Imitate

• Coach

Motivate

Never forget that people who are learning something need to see the benefits of doing so. We live in a WIIFM world – what's in it for me? I firmly believe that all trainers should also be salespeople at heart and always be willing and able to sell their training to anyone who cares to ask. It's so dangerous to assume everyone wants to be there on the course or to be at the receiving end of a training session. Many don't, and with today's choices, people can move on somewhere else if they wish.

We simply have to give some benefits to them of learning what we are going to teach them. That's why I made a point of giving you some benefits at the beginning of this article.

Let me give you an example of MEDIC in action, which I used just the other day with my eleven-year-old son Lewis. Now Lewis just loves boiled eggs, and he really loves mine. Now I can't cook anything else I'm afraid, just boiled eggs, but I do cook a vastly superior boiled egg. I thought it was time to teach my son how to do it. Sort of like passing skills on from father to son! I motivated him with a couple of benefits.

"Lewis, if you learn to boil an egg, this means that you can enjoy a perfect boiled egg whenever you wish. Also, the method I'll teach you will ensure you have that perfect, soft yolk that you love so much."

Explain

Whatever you're teaching will probably need some explanation. Sometimes we're teaching something that's quite technical, such as the laws relating to selling mortgages, or the process of overcoming objections in selling. So there needs to be some explaining. This is what we call in the business "chalk and talk", usually accompanied by a flip chart.

Here're some tips to help your explanation:

- Explain in a logical sequence.
- Ensure you're clear and concise.
- Don't rush.
- Use small, easily digestible chunks.
- Avoid jargon.
- Use questions to test understanding.
- Using visual aids to aid understanding.
- Use anecdotes, acronyms, stories - anything to make remembering easier.
- Make it interesting.

With the explanation, please get them to do it rather than you, especially if you are training a group of people. This is the cornerstone of accelerated learning – get them to do it. Set up an activity so they read up on the explanation and explain to each other. Give them a case study so they discover it themselves. Run a group discussion so the learned ones educate the non-learned ones. Allow a bit of trial and error. Run a group brainstorm to see how much they do know.

With my boiled eggs with Lewis, I broke down the explanation into four key steps and explained each one separately.

- Step 1 is to boil the water.

- Step 2 is to lower the egg into the water.

- Step 3 is to time for four minutes exactly.

- Step 4 (Might I say, the true secret, so don't tell anyone) is to remove the pan and pour cold water into the pan displacing the hot water. That way you stop the egg cooking.

Demonstration

Next comes the demonstration. Skills or processes or anything that involves doing something or saying something can be demonstrated. You, as the trainer, could do this. Or you could get someone else in to do it – maybe an expert, since you can't be an expert at everything. You could use a DVD or a media clip on your laptop.

Whoever does it is not the issue – it's how it's done. Here're some tips:

- Keep the demo visible.

- Demo in small stages.

- Use real equipment, forms, etc.

- Demo at an appropriate speed. Slower at first is best.

- Explain as you go.

- Allow time for questions.

And before you even start, do make sure you've practised.

Because I'd broken down my boiled egg steps into four stages, I was able to demonstrate each step to Lewis.

Imitation

Next comes the imitation. In training this is so important and, unfortunately, the bit often missed out on when time gets tight – and it always does.

When people practise something, they start to get things "in the muscle". It becomes second nature.

When I pull away at a junction in my car, yes, I move up the gears, but I don't recall doing it. I just do it instinctively – it's in my "muscle memory".

Role play is a typical imitation activity, or a case study, pictograms, cartooning, debates, group discussion, crosswords, a quiz, a test, a game. The list goes on.

Or you could just ask them to perform the skill in front of you to see that they can do it.

Coach

Whilst they're performing, that's when coaching comes in. Now coaching is a subject of many more articles. Suffice it to say that the art of coaching is to watch them, pause them, and ask how they're doing so far, what's going well, what's not going so well, what could they do differently. Only if necessary do you tell them where they've gone wrong.

It's very emotional learning something new. Inside us we feel threat and intimidation. When we don't know how to do something we get nervous, so go easy on the feedback. Imagine the delegate was you learning the skill. It's not easy. Encouragement gets more results than criticism.

Occasionally you'll want to get your learner to loop back to the explain or demonstrate bit again, maybe if they missed something, so be gracious to do this.

So there we have MEDIC – motivate, explain, demonstrate, imitate, and coach. Follow the steps whenever you put a training session together and you won't go far wrong.

As for Lewis and the boiled eggs, we got to the imitation stage and my wife walked in and interrupted the show. Claire said that Lewis is too young to boil water. She probably has a point.

I'm now grounded for a week!

How to Handle Challenging Learners

Six strategies to avoid conflict in the training room

Anyone involved in sales knows that the best way to deal with customer objections is to pre-empt them, in other words, prevent rather than cure.

Here're six strategies you can adopt right now to avoid any potential conflict in your training rooms.

Get some upfront agreement

We often use the phrase "contracting". Don't, it sounds like a lawyer and the formal contract. Not perhaps the right atmosphere to start a seminar with.

However, you do need to get things out in the open and agree on expectations of you and the course and the group. If the group decides the terms of engagement, then you can use this powerful force later on if any one individual is causing issues. The power of the group is paramount to your success.

During the engagement session, you'll see the positive and negative people, which will be useful for later. Positivity often wins over negativity.

An upfront agreement also allows you to make alterations to your course content, maybe more practical exercises and energisers, or give the group more smartphone breaks…whatever is needed, you be the judge.

WIIFM

Not a radio station broadcasting outside of L.A., but an acronym – what's in it for me?

If your group can't see any benefit in attending the seminar or listening to you, then they won't listen, and that might cause problems later. This is just exacerbated if they were told to come on the course, which still happens to every trainer.

People, learners, delegates, in fact, anyone is motivated by:

* Saving money

* Making money (bonuses, commission)

* Saving time

* Making their work easier

* Getting more done in the time available

So dig deep and tell them what the benefits are in attending right upfront, or even in the welcome pack you send them beforehand.

Seating

Last week my training room allocated to me was only big enough for a board table. Sometimes I've trained in room cupboards, in open offices…I'm sure you have too.

But if you can, choose the layout carefully and don't default to the traditional "U" shape. This was originally designed to cater to those big, boxlike OHPs we used back in the '80s and '90s, which used to stand in front of the U.

The world has moved on now and we don't need this setup. Where space allows, I like to opt for bistro style. My tag, which means lots of small tables or round tables or just two tables joined together to accommodate four or so people. Once you have this setup, the advantages are tremendous:

- It's easy to involve the whole group when you ask for something, i.e., each table acts like a mini-group rather than just one person taking charge.
- The small groups self-manage, i.e., they will handle the difficult person for you.
- It allows you to use more group work and exercises.
- It inspires competition amongst tables.
- It's very difficult in small groups for one person to 'opt-out'.

Team creating

Lots of activities and exercises, that's the answer to total involvement, and setting up teams or mini groups to conduct these exercises can sometimes lead to conflict, particularly when the group knows each other. So avoid people working with their pals, cliques being set up, people working with the same people.

I encourage movement of groups and team members, so to create groups try these:

- All those born in January to March on this table please…
- Height order to determine the groups.
- Deal out playing cards and all hearts on this table, clubs on this table…
- Number people – 1, 2, 3, 4 around the room to create teams at random.
- Ask them to work in teams with people that they haven't worked with before.
- Scorpios, Taureans, Sagittarians on this table please…

I'm sure you get the idea. Keep changing teams, encourage movement.

Team Leader

If you have groups larger than four people, then you need someone to become team leader or coordinator should you wish your activities to be finished on time. I always randomly choose a leader to prevent the toxic one taking over all the time.

Here're some ideas:

- The tallest person on the team
- The person who has been with the organisation for the longest time
- The person who lives the closest to this building in miles, etc.
- "The person wearing the most blue". You can use this tactic if you want a particular person to head the group – maybe the most positive person; just check what they're wearing first.

Movement

If the body ain't moving, the brain ain't grooving.

And movement can calm the frustrations of certain group members. So, keep things moving, including your learners. When learners are kept moving it increases their energy levels and adds curiosity and anticipation to the workshop, which keeps them ready to learn and less likely to look for the negative. After all, it's very difficult to be negative about something if you're feeling energised.

Fire and challenging learners

I was attending fire training the other day, learning how fires start and keep going. There are three elements to a fire – ignition, fuel, and oxygen – take any one away and it stops. But add more fuel or oxygen to the fire and it roars out of control.

In the same way, when you have hot 'n' spicy delegates on your courses or difficult people, we may add to the fire by adding fuel and oxygen.

For example, we're up against the "expert" who keeps telling the group how brilliant he is; we might fight this by trying to appear the expert ourselves and get into an ego battle.

Or we might be dealing with the chatterbox who won't stop chipping in. We try and talk even more to counteract them.

Or the "disagreeable" one who has some weird ideas and is totally negative. We might try to argue with him to prove our point or get defensive.

This just stokes the fire.

Instead we should remove one of the elements to diffuse them.

For the "expert" we give them the audience they seek, and let them become the expert to refer to when we're not quite sure of the exact detail.

The chatterbox, we can let them run out of steam and let the wrath of the group gobble them up. Or better still, learn to interrupt and summarise, then do the Traffic Police technique to stop them talking.

The "disagreeable" one is best left to the group. Let the group consume him by awarding power to the group to subsume him. Or the real biscuit…use the question, "I wonder what others think about Brian's thinking," and let the group absorb him.

Psychological Judo

Her name is Florence, and she's a gorgeous six-month-old Italian Spinone puppy. Always looking for attention, loves a cuddle, and dotes over the children.

But she's also a destructive nightmare. She chews anything in sight whilst her teeth are coming through. Chair legs, boxes of breakfast cereal, and cables. Anything is fair game for Florence.

So how have we dealt with it? Telling her off, putting things out of sight, putting her on the lead. Limited success until I started to use psychological judo.

For any of you who have done judo, you know that success comes by using the power of the opposition to overcome them. Don't play against the tide; work with the current. I couldn't stop Florence from chewing everything in sight, so why stop her?

A trip to the wood shed and I returned with four large logs that we would normally put on the wood burner. I dropped these around the conservatory where the dogs stay, and sure enough, Florence took to them instantly.

Of course, she made a mess, but the wood shavings and torn up strips of wood remained dry on the slate-tiled floor and were easily cleared up. Hey, presto, problem solved.

In the same way, this is how we should deal with tricky or challenging delegates on our courses and workshops. They're not going to act differently so why try to stop them? For example, you might have someone who keeps interrupting and trying to prove they know more than you on the subject, so don't get upset and stressed. Instead make them your co-trainer, the expert you can call upon to help with technical details. Just by recognising the yearning need of your tricky delegate, you can use this need to handle them.

Another example. You might have the doodler who can't stop themselves drawing doodles and pictures. Ask them to draw a picture to help summarise the session and display it on the wall for everyone to see. You could have the moaner who doesn't like the changes the company is going through as they've been around for a thousand years. Appoint them the course "sage" and ask for their opinions of how it used to be done and how it compares with now. Bear in mind, though, that you need to keep control of their "air" time.

Remember, don't fight fire with fire. Use psychological judo to handle your hot and spicy delegates. And very soon Florence's teeth will all be through, and she won't need to carry on chewing my logs. After all, I'm getting a little fed up with vacuuming every day.

The Joker

- Tells jokes and funny stories
- Makes fun of serious subjects and never misses a pun
- Mocks other delegates and makes innuendos

Ignore It. Use your own sense of humour to build on their humour.

Confront, especially if they are being rude. Talk to them during the break, explaining that others are sensitive.

Relay to group. When you reach a serious point, ask the group to say how our joker would make a joke about this one. Be honest with this one. For example, "So there we have the Financial Services and Markets Act and how we're regulated to protect the customer. How do you think Mike might view that?"

Psychological judo. Ask the joker for periodic humorous stories or anecdotes to summarise sessions. Appoint them as the workshop official joker to make light of all things. Give them a whistle to blow whenever they reach a point where they have to have a laugh. They'll soon stop.

The Texter

- Attached to their smartphone which keeps vibrating

- Keeps glancing at the phone to check texts and emails

- Occasionally puts on lap to send an email

Ignore it. This is what most trainers do.

Confront. Confront the whole group at the right time and agree what they want to do about smartphones. Maybe extra smartphone breaks every hour, say five minutes.

Contract with the group. If you sense that smartphones may dominate, run a short contracting session with the group in the morning to agree what they expect from you the trainer, and what the group expect of themselves.

Psychological judo. Build into the sessions the use of their smartphones:

1. When doing roleplay, you could create a telephone-based scenario and get them to role play this using their smartphones. All you need to do is ask them to write their mobile numbers on the white board and pair them off.

1. Use an SMS polling software whereby they can use their phones to enter a poll and have the results displayed up on the big screen. I use http://www.smspoll.net/

2. Ask them to text you questions rather than asking in person. This works well for large groups when people might be intimidated to ask normally. Have the questions display on the big screen. Naturally you can put out a hashtag and get them to tweet instead, but not everyone tweets – believe me they don't – but most people text.

3. Every now and then ask the group to Google a fact or something. Ensure this comes over as part of your plan, not because you don't know the answer. Have a small prize for the person who comes up with the answer first.

4. Put up a brief quiz on the screen and let them Google the answers.

5. Have them phone their phones to leave a message the next time you're doing vocal training or presentation skills, so they can hear themselves.

6. Test their listening skills when on the phone, by allowing them to phone a friend in the room and listen. You can even have the call recorded and pinged to their email inbox as a sound file, for listening later. Email me if you want to know how.

7. Use the audio and video record functions of their phones by asking groups to create a mini movie. It could be to summarise some of their key learnings from the day or to illustrate a topic from the course schedule. Have them create the video and ask them to upload to a video channel you've just created on YouTube or to their own channel. Fire up YouTube on your laptop and view.

Griper

- Always negative and complains about everything

- Was sent on the workshop, didn't want to come.

- Whinges constantly

Relay their points to the group by "hamming them up out of all proportion". For example, the Griper whinges about how awful the quotes look on the printer. You reply, "What you're saying then is that the quotes look absolutely awful and they'll never work at all and that customers actually hate them." Turn to the group and say, "Do we all agree?" The group's positive attitude and possible anger at the Griper will encourage them to rally round you.

Psychological judo. Appoint them as the Workshop Devil's Advocate. Ask them to blow the whistle whenever they hear or see something that just won't work or other negative things triggered by the workshop. The effort of blowing the whistle may prevent them from being negative. Alternatively ask them to make a list of all the negative items and present their findings to the group at the end of each session. This does work and should encourage the group to argue the case with him.

Expert

- Wants to be recognised

- Wants the spotlight and knows as much as you if not more

- Interrupts to point out mistakes and disagrees with facts given

Reverse questions. Use the reverse technique to ensure they answer their own questions, which, invariably, are statements designed to show the group how intelligent they are.

Relay questions. When dealing with a particularly difficult question from another delegate, ricochet the question to the expert. Don't come across as if you are testing him. Emphasise that we all need his help (genuinely).

Don't confront. You'll never win.

Psychological judo. Treat as co-leader. Consult him during the break as confidential "assistant". Recognise him in the capacity as technical expert. Appoint him as some form of monitor to channel his energy. For example, make him the "Facts Man" by asking him to verify all facts and information for their correctness. Give him a whistle to blow whenever he needs to stop the group to comment.

Eager Beaver

- Keeps trying to help but whose contributions "miss the mark"

- Embarrasses other delegates with his constant interruption and unfortunate contributions

Seek relevance. Ask them to reframe their contribution. "Help me to see where your point fits in with printing quotations professionally."

Confront. Make it clear to them that you know they are trying to help but that you would like contributions from everyone.

Speak to them during the break for their help in letting others contribute.

Doodler

- Makes elaborate drawings on note paper whilst you're talking

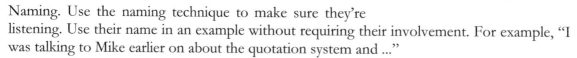

Ignore. It's probably a sign of concentration. Some people prefer to doodle rather than watch you. It doesn't mean they are not listening.

Naming. Use the naming technique to make sure they're listening. Use their name in an example without requiring their involvement. For example, "I was talking to Mike earlier on about the quotation system and ..."

Refocus their attention with the flip chart.

Psychological judo. Ask them to be the group's cartoonist by drawing a picture for each session run which could be used to summarise the session for the group. Pin the picture to the wall.

Caveman

- Unwillingness to question own beliefs

- Makes "black and white" statements

- Doesn't like new thinking

Reflect to group. Confirm their views by stating, "What you're saying is that there's nothing wrong with the old way of doing things." "How does the rest of the group feel?" Peer pressure from the group should undermine him.

Confront. Confirm with him that the purpose of the workshop is to examine new ways of doing things and gain agreement that we should let others contribute.

Tell a story. Tell a story or parable to the group of someone who never changed and the consequences. Address the story to the group at the beginning of a session and the message will soon strike home.

Psychological judo. Appoint them as the "Chairman of the Business" and ask them to speak up whenever they feel the workshop is discussing something unrealistic or unethical. The impact of this peer pressure will keep them quiet.

Heckler

- Probably insecure

- Aggressive and argumentative

- Interprets new ideas as attacks on him

Never get upset yourself.

Naming technique - Pre-empt their aggression by naming them in a situation. E.g., let's imagine James has begun to print off a new style quote, what problems would he have? By pre-empting their reservation you are channelling their energies positively.

Psychological judo. This type of person is easy to identify quickly, and using judo you can overcome them. For example, if they will not participate in syndicate exercises, announce to the group that later on we'll be doing some syndicate work but that some of you may not be able or want to participate.

Ask those to see you at lunchtime before the exercises. When your challenger approaches you, emphasise the nature of the exercise and encourage them not to participate. Human nature will make him participate later.

Shy Violet

- Avoids eye contact and blushes easily

- Speaks rarely and in a low voice

- Never volunteers information

Questions. Give them easy, closed questions to encourage them to be confident.

Naming. Use their name in examples to build their confidence.

Psychological judo. Start a new session announcing to the whole group, "This session is very participative and the only way it'll work is if we have contributions from everyone. I realise that some people don't like to contribute. They'd rather listen and take it all in. If you feel you're rather shy, that's okay as there are others who'll make up for this."

Speedy Gonzalez

- Finishes exercises well before the others

- Is impatient with slower group members

- Wants to move on when all are not ready

Confront. Ask for his patience by explaining that others may need more time.

Tell a story. Use the story method to tell a parable about the tortoise and the hare to the group.

Psychological judo. Give them a complex task to finish quickly. Appoint them as group "pacer" and to blow a whistle when he's finished because you know he'll finish first. The group will soon shut him up. Give him two exercises rather than the one that the group receives. Make it known that he's fast and recognise him. With such a spotlight and peer pressure, he'll soon withdraw to run at the group's speed.

Trapper

- Wants to trap you constantly

- Jumps in to interrupt when you slip up

- Points out inconsistencies in your argument or approach

Own up. Admit you were wrong and thank them for identifying the "problem".

Relay to group. Paraphrase his point and exaggerate it and pass onto the group for their comments (look for support!). For example, "So what you're saying is that I'm ignoring his point of view when I state this Company Procedure. In fact, I'm totally avoiding this?".. pause..."Does anyone else support this view?"

Psychological judo. Appoint them as group "Watchdog" whose job is to blow a whistle and place a red card in the air whenever they see an inconsistency or a fault in the presentation or material. Put pressure on them to find fault. Put the spotlight on them.

Whisperer

• Makes whispered comments to neighbour

Non-verbal. (Most powerful). Look at them deadpan, say nothing, and wait patiently. When they look at you, wink at them or mouth, "Okay." They'll either share the remark they've made or shut up in the future.

Psychological judo. At the beginning of a session, confirm to the group that we've got a lot to cover over the next idea. Ask that anyone who has difficulty keeping up with the flow should ask their neighbour for assistance. So long as they whisper and don't interrupt everyone else, that's fine with you.

Yawner

• Yawns, stifles yawns

• Eyelids droop

Naming. Use their name in an example to make them sit up and listen.

Non-verbal. When they catch your eye, nod at them or wink at them to show them that you're aware of their condition.

Call a break. During the break, examine the workshop content to allow more activity.

Psychological judo. Put the spotlight on our friend. For example, "After lunch we're going to see a really good video. Some of you, mainly the older ones who can't take the pressure, might want to use this opportunity for a bit of shut-eye. The rest of us will enjoy this excellent video" (said jokingly).

Watch out for John

It was the summer of 1993. I was running a small training team with UK-wide delivery targets, and I was up to deliver a sales training workshop to advisers in the Southwest region, a very successful region, well-managed with a variety of characters to keep me busy.

"Watch out for John" was the warning from the regional manager. "He doesn't want to be there, detests training, and winds everyone up. Be careful. He could wreck the workshop."

Gulp, I thought, how do I handle this nightmare or, as I prefer to call them, hot 'n' spicy delegates.

I took some advice from a wise and knowledgeable mentor trainer, and he told me about the red and yellow card system.

All trainers have hot 'n' spicy delegates on our workshops, especially if you're in the corporate environment where you might have people being sent on courses who don't particularly want to be there.

And all trainers have tried confronting these delegates both in and out of the classroom – this never works. The group soon rallies around their delegate. They won't side with you; you're an outsider. There are tricks and secrets in handling each one and I'll share these later, but for now, let's focus on my friend from the Southwest.

The trick is to realise that many of these delegates are a nuisance to you, but they are also an irritation to others on the course who want to get on and learn. So you use the power of the group to subdue them.

That's where the yellow and red card system comes in.

During the introduction to my course in Newton Abbot in 1993, I played on the fact that today we're only looking at practical sales ideas and I promised I wouldn't be wallowing in theory. I always say this because wallowing deep in theory serves no purpose. Salespeople attend training to stock up on new ideas.

I went on to explain that we'd be moving at a good pace to ensure they all received plenty of value. Salespeople like this kind of approach. Then out came my pack of yellow and red cards, and as I dished these out to everyone, I continued to explain that whenever someone says or does something that is not helping, or going off subject, or not relevant to today's objective, they can be yellow-carded. And that includes me as well. The red card is for a second offence, and if you get one of these, you have to pay the penalty. All said with a smile and a wink—people get the idea.

So now you have the group on the side of the workshop, not on your side but behind practical learning that gives them value and results.

You can imagine what happened when my friend started piping up, can't you? The group was ready for him. Remember, they all knew each other and were expecting him to react that day as he had in countless courses before. The yellow cards were a little slow at first, but my friend soon got the message, and he was a little angel for the rest of the day.

I've used the cards often since that time. Sometimes I'll introduce them in the afternoon session if I've come across some tricky characters in the morning. It never fails.

Try it. Order some coloured cards from your stationers. Cut them up into small cards and keep them in a plastic sleeve in your pilot case.

Controlling the Training Environment

Now I must have run training courses and spoken to audiences in hundreds of different rooms, ranging from huge conference halls to tiny cupboards, rooms with beautiful views across vast countryside or cityscapes, to rooms with no windows and just fluorescent lights.

As a trainer, we all like our favourite layout. Sometimes you don't have a choice, but where we do or can influence the layout, here're a few thoughts to help you decide what is best for you and your programme.

U Shape

The traditional U shape is a standard for most courses so is non-threatening. Delegates have a table to rest their workbooks, glasses, water, name cards, etc. Often they have enough space although some hotels are notorious for squeezing people into the tiniest of spaces.

Next time you have a U shape, watch how each delegate creates their own space around their table. Items are strategically placed to mark out their territory.

Here's a small room with the U shape fatter rather than thinner. This allows more space for the trainer in general so he/she can interact with the learners. It also allows for the visuals to be closer to the group.

The opposite here with a thinner U shape which allows more people in the room. Not a lot of space between the learners and the wall and little space for the trainer to walk into the U.

It allows the trainer to move into the U to encourage involvement, and all delegates can see the trainer and any visuals that are being used. Be careful to place the screen to either side of the U, not in the middle, as is usually the default. Screens in the middle dominate and mean the trainer must stand to one side of the U, which rather defeats the object really.

The tables do create a barrier between the trainer and delegate but not insurmountable.

Some smaller rooms don't allow for a U shape, and where one is created, the tables tend to nudge the walls of the room and make it difficult for delegates to get out, or maybe that's the idea!

You can have long, thin U's or short, fat U's.

Did you admire the 1990s old box projector at the front? That shot was taken in 2001.

A long, thin room, not ideal, especially with the screen dominating the front of the room. Notice the chairs have arms – much more comfortable for sitting in for long periods.

A well-spread-out U shape giving maximum room for the trainer to get close to the group. Notice the laptop and projector over on the far right-hand corner. The downside is that the delegates on either end of the U are a long way away from each other.

Boardroom

Here there is a large table, which can cause a barrier between the learner and the facilitator and can appear very formal. Boardrooms across the nation are usually occupied with a large hardwood, very shiny board table, which will not budge. They were designed for meetings and not really training sessions. Some delegates are a long way from the trainer, which might actually suit them.

A small boardroom set out as a syndicate room. Nice and modern with visual aids on the wall. Ideal for small group work.

A larger room here with tables stacked together to make a board table. Good for group discussion work.

If you find yourself in a boardroom with a huge board table, there's very little you can do about it. Here are a couple of things to do to allow some flexibility.

Before people arrive, remove the chairs from the left-hand corner at the front so you can base yourself there rather than from right at the front. This gives you some manoeuvrability, and it also allows delegates to see the visuals, which are usually located right bang at the front.

To encourage group discussion, sit down and remain at their level. The board table was designed so that everyone could see each other and contribute to meetings. Here're a few more examples of boardroom layouts

An enormous board table impossible to move. Great for peripheral visual aids to be placed in the middle of the table and lots of room for toys and fiddlies. Don't dare to stick things on the wall, though, as the wallpaper is usually very plush in boardrooms.

Standard board table in a purpose-built training room. Looks smart and can fit a fair few people around the table. Shame they didn't put a U shape in when they fitted the room.

Bistro

I like bistro, otherwise known as min tables. You need a fair-sized room to have three or four or maybe more round tables scattered around just like a bistro restaurant. Bistro is ideal for teamwork courses or highly interactive game/activity-based workshops as they encourage lots of participation and allow the trainer to mingle amongst the tables just like a waiter. Teams can occupy a whole table, and everyone can talk and listen to each other.

Typical bistro layout here. Three or four delegates per table with bodies occupying one-half of the table when the trainer is presenting and space to spread out when they're doing syndicate work. Space for drinks and things and space to move between the tables—a good layout.

Rectangular tables made into bistro tables. Not ideal as quite dangerous to move around the room with corners jutting out. They all seem to be working hard though.

Little more congested here with each table having about five or six bodies, but still lots of room, and lots of delegate involvement.

However, it is not good for formal presentations or when using visual aids as some learners may not be able to see. It's typically what you'll have if you're doing any after-dinner presentations. You need a big room to accommodate the tables.

Theatre

Theatre style is the typical layout when you want to fit lots of people into a room. More suited to formal presentations rather than training sessions as it's difficult to get learner involvement since there's usually a big distance between them and the trainer. If there is no gradient in the room, then it might be difficult for people at the back to see the presenter, although this problem goes away when you use university-type lecture theatres which resemble the old Roman theatres. Great, though, for packing people in, and if you've created fire escape channels (which you should) the presenter could walk up this corridor and get closer to the audience.

Here you'll notice the fire escape corridor up the middle and name badges on delegates—and a lot of people in a small space.

If you're presenting and using visual aids, keep the screen to one side of the presentation area so you can occupy the central position, and make sure you use a wireless remote so you can change slides wherever you are.

Tricky for name cards so name badges are usually preferred. Be careful with cups and glasses being knocked over – check the hotel to see who has to pay for spillages!

No tables

One of my favourite layouts where the subject is communication or body language or presentation skills.

A little scary for most people when they walk in. But once they get used to it, they feel more open and inclusive. There are no barriers between the trainer and the delegates so rapport can be built very quickly.

They do look relaxed, don't they? No barriers. Handouts are causing a few people some problems as writing on paper on your lap is tricky.

A cross between theatre and no tables, but again, no barrier between trainer and delegates.

Make sure any material is bound in workbook format so this can rest on their laps – handouts are a no-no.

Name badges rather than name cards work well. Overtones of touchy-feely group sessions.

Outside

Lovely if the sun is shining, but delegates can get easily distracted. Use selectively for syndicate exercises or sessions where teams need to achieve a task. Can revitalise delegates.

The sun's shining, and this gives people energy to work. Ideal for a twenty-minute syndicate exercise. Mine's a pint of bitter.

Outside again, beautiful setting and this will revitalise the delegates.

Toys and activities

As a trainer it is vital for you to be able to identify which areas of the course will be dry and tedious for the group, so that you can find a creative way to present the information, which will then lead to enhanced learning.

Try creating some fun and laughter. Some trainers dismiss games and activities as time wasters or childish. Yet this is the best way to deliver complex information, far better than having delegates fall asleep through boredom, or worse still, reduced to tears because they feel so overwhelmed by the complexity!

The average adult passive attention span is about twenty minutes. Taking a break every half hour would be disruptive. Instead, use a quick brainteaser or energiser, a short trivia quiz, or a course-related puzzle.

The time before lunch can be a seriously low-energy time for delegates. Avoid videos here as this encourages the delegates to snooze, particularly if the lights are lowered. Keep the energy moving with a very active group exercise after the mid-morning break – skill practice would be good here; put sweets and treats out on tables, plus small 'toys' for them to play with, e.g., Lego pieces, Koosh balls, puzzles, tactile children's toys.

Put more toys out for the afternoon break. Try yo-yos and Frisbees. Most people can't resist having a go, remembering what it felt like as a child - which helps to utilise right-brain learning during the session.

Use the toys to assist the actual content delivery. A fun quiz can be made more enjoyable by asking learners to use some of the larger toys as part of the quiz.

Music

I'm often asked about the role of music in the training environment. Does it help? Is it just a gimmick? Is one type of music better than another? There has been a lot of research carried out on the effectiveness of music in learning - I do believe music has a role in the training room. It can be used for:

- Prior to start - makes the training room more inviting for learners to enter, helping break down barriers and fears, as well as setting the tone for the workshop

- Break time - makes the training room 'friendlier' for those learners who stay in the room during that time

- Socialisation - bringing learners together

- State changer - helps manage learner states as specific music can enhance precise states for learning

- Priming - to prepare the learner for the next learning experience

- Movement - to get learners up and moving

- Emotions - to aid bringing emotions into learning

- Calming - to slow and calm the mind and body down

Beware the use of music when learners are trying to concentrate - it can interfere/compete with the attention system   Also beware of using music for more than ten to fifteen minutes at any one time - learners will become habitualised to it, and it will lose its impact.

Sizzling Session Starters

- "Wake Up (It's a Beautiful Morning)" – (Boo Radleys)
- "Oh! What a Beautiful Morning" - *Oklahoma* soundtrack
- Theme From *2001: A Space Odyssey*
- Epic film soundtracks such as *E.T., Superman, Chariots of Fire*

Breaks

- "An American in Paris" - (Gershwin)
- Polkas
- "Fun, Fun, Fun" – (Beach Boys)
- "Shout" - (Lulu)

Games/Simulations

- Piano rags - (Scott Joplin)
- "The Sorcerer's Apprentice" - (Dukas)

Captivating Closes

- "We are the Champions" - (Queen)
- "Celebrate" - (Madonna)
- "I've Had the Time of My Life" - *Dirty Dancing* soundtrack
- "Simply the Best" - (Tina Turner)
- Try introducing music when your learners arrive and at breaks.

The beat drives you on... and on

Battling to raise yourself off the sofa now that the miserable weather and dark nights have set in? If the gym seems a distant memory, researchers believe the key to rekindling your enthusiasm for exercise could come from Robbie Williams or Whitney Houston.

The Spice Girls could stimulate you into plodding an extra 10 minutes on the treadmill and that evergreen Welsh crooner Tom Jones might give you enough energy to take up salsa dancing.

Sports psychologists at Brunel University in London, who have been studying for 10 years the psychological and physical effects that music has on exercise and sports performance, say that listening to certain tunes can boost your activity output. Dr Costas Karageorghis, a senior lecturer, has found that the right melodies not only inspire people to get their trainers on but also help them to work out for longer. "Music boosts emotional and physical arousal levels and can be used as a stimulant prior to any sort of physical exercise. It also acts as a sedative, calming you down after a stressful day so that you are more in the mood to work out."

Music has this effect because of the way we interpret it. Unconsciously, explains Dr Karageorghis, we store up mental images associated with the songs we find most inspiring or soothing. When they are played, they automatically trigger the images in our minds. "The theme to the *Rocky* films is a typical example of how this works. Immediately we hear it, we think of Sylvester Stallone training hard in pursuit of his dream. That is enough to stimulate some people into heading out for a run."

While you are working out, the best time to plug in the headset is when you are beginning to flag. "In our studies, we have shown that people who listen to music while running or cycling can extend their workout times by up to 15 per cent," he says. "As they tire, music diverts their attention from their fatigue. It alters their perception of how hard they are working so that they keep going for longer."

The therapeutic effects of music are well accepted within the medical profession. Psychologists at Strathclyde University proved that listening to music helped speed the recovery time of women undergoing operations at the Western Infirmary in Glasgow.

At the University of California, pupils who were asked to perform spatial reasoning tests 10 minutes after listening to Mozart's *Sonata for Two Pianos in D Major* scored 30 per cent higher marks than those who listened to more repetitive music or who simply sat in silence.

Pauline Etkin, director of the Nordoff-Robins music

....

'When natural rhythms are off kilter, listening to music can help restore balance'

therapy centre in north London, says music is so soothing because, throughout life's ups and downs, our ability to listen and respond to harmony and rhythm remains unimpaired. "Music's rhythm is closely linked with the rhythms of the body. When someone is nervous, afraid or suffering in any way and their natural rhythms are thrown off kilter, listening to music can help restore the balance."

This rhythmic link with the body's movements is important in fitness, too. By synchronising mind and body, music can make exercise seem easier and more enjoyable. "That is the reason why aerobics, circuits and other classes set to music are so popular," Dr Karageorghis says. "Focus on a strong beat and your body will try to embrace it."

In international sport, this principle was put to the test this year, when Britain's first athletics event set to music was staged at the National Indoor Arena in Birmingham. At the Aqua Pura Indoor Spectacular, high jumpers, triple jumpers and long jumpers competed with their favourite tracks blaring out from the sound system. "The athletes got to choose a piece of music which they thought would inspire them to jump higher or further," says Jon Ridgeon, spokesman for Fastrack, the organiser of the meeting.

"The Ethiopian runner Haile Gebreselassie asked for *Scatman*, a techno track, to be played during a race in Birmingham, where he set the World Indoor record for 2,000 metres. And at some outdoor track meetings we arrange for African drum bands to play during the endurance events. Runners find it useful to hear a fast rhythm beating in the background."

For others, it is the lyrics of a song, rather than the tempo, that have proved instrumental in their success.

Dr Karageorghis's colleague Professor Peter Terry accompanied Great Britain's bobsleigh team to the 1998 Winter Olympics in Japan. As the squad's sport psychologist, his job was to ensure they believed they could win Britain's first medal in the event since 1964. "Every day when they approached the bob track for training and also on competition days, the team would listen to Whitney Houston's *One Moment In Time* while visualising themselves calmly and decisively seizing their moment. On the final race day, that's exactly what they did and took the bronze medal."

Your own mix should put you in a positive mood and energise you. Ideally, you should select songs that you associate with physical activity. But if you really want to make history on your run around the park this evening, tune in to Vangelis's theme music to *Chariots of Fire*. "It conjures up visions of Olympic glory, and the ability to walk on air," says Dr Karageorghis. "For most people who struggle to set foot out of the door, that one usually does the trick."

Using Music in Training – the Laws

Do you want to use music in your training? Would you like to be able to play any MP3, CD, or tape? If so, you'll need to be covered by both a PRS & PPL licence, even if you're streaming from Spotify in a classroom or playing a YouTube video.

Unless you purchase CDs or tapes that are royalty-paid (both in respect of the artists and the production company), then you will need the licences detailed below.

Performing Right Society (PRS) Licence

PRS pays money to the writers and publishers of music. Usually they license the premises so, if you train at hotels and conference venues, check with the venue to see if they already have the licence. If not, you can obtain your own licence as a trainer that will be valid wherever you train.

If, however, your training is run on your company's own premises, then your company will need to obtain the licence for the premises. This can either be obtained as an annual licence or you can pay per training course.

Phonographic Performance Limited (PPL) Licence

PPL pays money to record companies, recording artists, and musicians. As with the PRS licence, the most common application is to licence premises. If, however, the venue that you are training in does not have a licence, then you can purchase an individual trainer's licence that will cover you wherever you train. For in-house training, the office premises will need to be licensed – this fee is calculated depending on the square-metre space of the room used.

For further information on both licences, visit:

PRS – www.prs.co.uk

PPL – www.ppluk.com

The Secret of Smell in the training room

I'm going to share with you a neat way of always being in control of your state of mind. Imagine that—being able to change your state of mind at will.

For those who know me well, you know that I love dogs. I have two dogs, mother and daughter, Spinones, who are gun dogs, bred to sniff out birds and game in the rough ground, disturb them for the guns to shoot, and then retrieve the game for the gunner's pot later that evening. This breeding has been going on for centuries.

As a result my two dogs have a masterful sense of smell; I've heard it's a thousand times better than ours. The thing about smells is that they have no barriers to recollect the memory.

Have you a favourite smell that just triggers the memory associated with it? Maybe a perfume that reminds you of your first love or the smell of freshly cut grass which brings back lazy, hazy summer days.

Now that's the secret to managing your state of mind. Here's the strategy.

Make a note of the various states you need to perform optimally.

Maybe it's patience, maybe positivity, maybe curiosity.

Now think back to a time in the past where you had this state in abundance.

Relive the memory, but this time try and associate a smell or taste. If you can, the mere whiff of this smell will flood you back to that time and inject you with the state that you had at the time.

I have a few of examples:

- For a relaxing, totally comfortable state – I smell sun tan lotion – this brings back memories of lying on the beach without a care in the world.

- Fresh-cut grass helps me to inject myself with perseverance and finishing a boring job. As a teenager I earned most of my beer money cutting people's grass.

- To perform my best when in front of an audience I use saffron. This brings back memories of Iran when I had my first standing ovation.

- For clarity I use the smell of cold air. This memory is when I walk the dogs early in the morning when it's fresh and chilled and the air smells wonderful. My head feels totally clear and I ooze clarity.

It works—worth trying, nothing to lose.

The Fantastic Mr. Flip Chart

Portable, engaging, spontaneous, easy to use, colourful…the humble flip chart is experiencing a resurgence, and who can blame it? The flipchart, if used well, is a first-class training tool to captures the group's ideas, can be used to build your own ideas, and can be enormously visual with just a little cartoon training.

It's this building of ideas, pictures, bullets that engages the audience. We just become glued to a moving feast of information. It's the animation that engrosses us. What it's not is a medium to prepare a presentation. That's the domain of PowerPoint or Prezi.

Tips to use the humble flip chart

- If you want to use the flip chart for capturing words and bullets, follow the 1:3:6 rule. One topic per sheet, six lines maximum, and three words per line. Otherwise your group won't be able to read it as it'll be too small.

- If you're using the flip chart in a larger group with theatre-style seating, avoid writing in the bottom third of the chart as people won't be able to see.

- Use vivid colours because you can. Black and blue are the most readable. Use red to underline or bring attention to key points. Pinks, purples all work. However, green, yellow, orange just don't, so refrain from even getting them out of the box.

- Use chisel point pens as these are far more readable than pointed flip chart pens.

- Invest well in pens. Check them before you leave and make sure the ones in your pilot case have plenty of ink. Don't rely on those provided by the venue; they're often dry.

- If you have a complex diagram to show or need prompting, you can draw a feint pencil image or words to remind you. Do this in the top corner and your group won't notice.

- Check the time on your watch from behind the easel so the group doesn't see you. And you do remove any clock in the room, don't you?

- Stick your running notes on the back of the easel to keep yourself on track.

- Make your flip very visual. Use cartoons, images, icons, drawings. Learn to draw in a basic fashion; the group doesn't expect you to be brilliant, and get over wanting to be professional. Google Graham Shaw. He does a fabulous book and online learning on how to draw cartoons.

- Buy flip pads that have feint perforations so you can rip off sheets and stick them to the walls. Better still, buy paper that has feint lines to keep your writing straight.

- When writing bullets of the flip, lower your body as you go to ensure your lines don't start sloping downwards.

- Refrain from holding onto pens or even worse still, conducting the group with your flip pen baton. Just put them down.

- Remember to touch, turn, and then talk. Never talk to the flip chart unless you have a lavaliere microphone strapped to your lapel.

Positioning your flip chart

- If you're right-handed, then position your easel to your left.

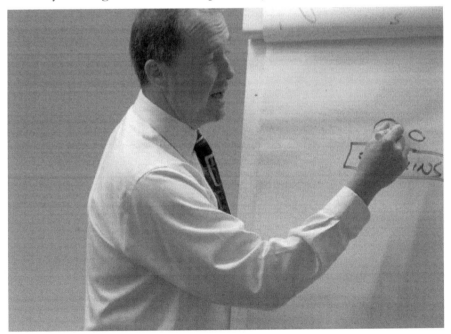

- Have two flip charts on both your left and right to help capture more information. This can maximise your spatial anchoring because you can aid your group to relate the flip charts to different things. For example, the one on your right can be for capturing group thoughts, and the one on the left can be for your input. Just walking to the right-hand flip chart will stir the group to remember to give you information and ideas.

- Give syndicate groups paper to capture the results of their syndicate work and stick them to the wall as they present.

- Use thin masking tape to stick the flips to the wall. Don't use Blu-Tack; that is a crime against humanity and walls.

- Store your pads sideways, not lengthways, to prevent the rippling effect, and if you can, store them flat rather than leaning against the wall.

Types of flip chart

- The traditional chart sits astride a metal easel fixed to the ground with three legs. Easily moved and lightweight.

- Wheeled models are particularly good for portability and can save your back.

- Half-sized flip charts are useful for small groups.

- Wall charts that hang from wall railings save space but are difficult to use.

- Whiteboards are glorified flip charts and, in my opinion, the best visual aid available. The rules are the same, but make sure you use dedicated whiteboard pens, otherwise you'll be there until the early hours trying to clean them. If you do use the wrong pen and it won't wipe, just run over the offending writing with a whiteboard pen, leave for fifteen minutes, and wipe off as normal.

- Whiteboards come in all sorts of shapes and sizes, can be fixed to the wall, or can have wheels for portability. A recent invention allows you to peel them out of a box and stick them on the wall. Imagine cling-film and think whiteboard and you can see this new invention. Clever and allows a whiteboard anywhere.

Three Great Ways to End a Programme

How difficult is it to change?

This exercise can and does work with groups ranging from six to 600 and is an excellent way of driving home the point that changing is difficult. It is used to encourage seminar participants to take action and make some changes that will affect their lives. Many speakers use words to say this point, but this exercise proves the point with action.

Ask the group to pair off male to male and female to female and find some space around the floor. Once they are ready—and this can take some time—announce the instructions. With a very large audience, you may wish to put the instructions on a slide.

Ask them to choose two items of clothing or accessories and swap them with the other person. Initially people will be reticent, but most will soon get into the spirit.

Once the noise dies down, ask the group how difficult it was to change. Encourage feedback if you have a small enough group or announce the difficulties if you have a large group. People will all agree that changing is a challenge.

Make your point now that as a result of the seminar, you have been learning many things and it's important to take action and change the way you act or perform to ensure all the valuable things you've learnt are put into practice.

Now carefully ask them to take their seats again. You will notice that virtually everyone will re-exchange their items with the other person before they sit down.

When everyone is comfortable, ask them why they returned their items to the other person, since strictly speaking you didn't ask them to do so. People will be a little embarrassed, and now you should make the point that change can be done but it is very easy to go back to the way things always were. We must ensure that any change we make continues and becomes second nature, like wearing your own clothes.

A neat exercise that will take about ten minutes, depending on the size of your group.

Who Wants the Tenner

This is a very simple exercise that'll last a few minutes, if that, but has an incredible effect.

Towards the end of your seminar, hand up a £10 note (or fiver if it's close to payday). Ask the question carefully, "Who wants this tenner?" Your audience will all put up their hands politely, and occasionally someone will walk up towards you and take it.

Occasionally you have to encourage people to take it since it's polite not to, and most people are polite.

Once someone has taken the tenner, applaud this person as they have taken action. Sometimes we literally have to get off our bottoms and make the changes that will affect our lives. Nobody else will do it for you, and results don't come on a platter. Waiting and sitting doesn't always get you results.

I have occasionally colour photocopied a ten-pound note, and this works really well as most people can't see the detail. However, the person who grabs it will be a little cheesed off. By the way, it is illegal to photocopy money so be careful!

The Seven-Day Sprint

This is a slight variation on our traditional action planning that most of us do at the end of seminars but is rather clever.

Draw on a flip chart or whiteboard a box with six boxes within. Something like this:

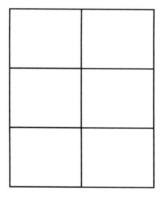

Ask the group to re-create this shape in their workbook or piece of paper. You are going to give them a seven-day sprint, and they must complete each box during the next seven days.

Now start putting the headings for each box. The headings can vary according to the programme you are running. For sales you might use:

1. Prospecting
2. Selling more
3. Social
4. Family
5. Me
6. Contact

As you write each one on the board, explain further what they need to write in the box. Prospecting here would mean that they need to write an idea in the box which will get them a new customer. 'Social' would be one thing they're going to do socially; 'family' is one hour of quality time with the whole family; 'me' could be one thing that you're going to do personally; 'contact' could be one person they have lost touch with, to get back in contact. No regrets, just get back in contact.

Here's a finished example:

Prospecting	More Sales
Family	Contact
Me	Social

Further explain that they need to complete each box in a week, i.e., seven days. After the first week, they can change the headings if they wish, or continue with a fresh box.

People have all commented to me how motivational this has been for them. Encourage your group to do this and take it forward in their lives so they can benefit from positive action.

Evaluation and Review

Reviewing your learnings

So often facilitators use only one review and do this at the end of the day (because learners don't like to review, and of course, we are short of time). However, it's vital for learners to be constantly reviewing new information/skills that have been encountered. Without it, the connections we have built up in the brain (neural networks of connected brain cells) simply drift apart, weakening the learning. Limit content in the workshop, but never compromise learning by reducing review time.

We need to think of creative ways to review so that we don't introduce it by saying, "Let's review." We also need to build in reviews every hour (maybe just a couple of minutes) and longer reviews after a break, lunch, or the start of a second day.

Ideally the review should be done in a different way from the way the information was originally encountered, building more pathways to the information as well as strengthening the original pathways. In other words, if the original information was learned in an auditory mode by learner discussions, for instance, then make the review a somatic experience by ensuring the review is bodily active or review in a visual manner with learners, maybe mind mapping the new information. There are hundreds of ways of doing this.

I would like to offer a couple of suggestions that I have found work particularly well and can be applied to any type of workshop. Not only do learners review the new learning, but also they change their state to a positive state for further learning by adding movement.

Example Reviews

The Twitter Review

A useful review exercise or one for the first activity in the morning. Explain how Twitter works, 140 characters to get your message across. Ask the group to prepare to tweet about...that's up to you and your topic. I've used them for:

1. Reviewing the main learning points from yesterday
2. The value proposition of the company
3. The main benefits of the product
4. What they think of the course so far

And if you have some serious Gen Y's in the room, you could set up a hashtag for your programme and start tweeting about the event and set up a sixty-inch TV to feed the stream in real time…or you might not.

A-Z of "Enter your course title here"

Prepare a flip chart (or several if you are working with a large group) with A-M down the left-hand side and N-Z down the middle and a heading "A-Z of Microsoft Access".

Form groups.

Provide each learner with a coloured marker pen.

Ask them to write a keyword/idea next to each letter of the alphabet on the flip chart. (You may need to suggest that they can be creative with a few of the letters if there is nothing appropriate for them.)

Advertise It

Ask learners to form groups of five to six.

Ask them to brainstorm fifteen key points from the workshop so far.

Ask them to then nominate the top three.

Ask them to then decide upon the top one.

With the top one, ask them to advertise it by ... (you can now choose from, a colourful poster, a radio jingle, a television advertisement, a 'stop press' newspaper article, etc.)

Allow twenty minutes for them to prepare.

Have teams then present their advertisement to the other groups.

Twitter review.

Explain how Twitter works; bear in mind most people know. It allows for a maximum of 140 characters in a message to be posted.

Ask the learners to create a Twitter post to explain to the world what they have learnt on the course.

Ask them to read out their tweets.

I Discovered

Objective: Review key information from the training.

Before the training, write these phrases on a flip cart or slide. At the training, ask participants to write one or more phrases on an index card and finish the sentence.

Phrases:

- I discovered
- I relearned
- I was surprised to learn
- I forgot that
- I noticed that
- I plan to
- I will tell colleagues about

Ask them to circulate and share what they wrote.

Call time and ask a few people to report back on something interesting they heard from someone else.

Index Card Review

Hand out index cards to each learner.

At the end of the morning ask learners to reflect and write onto the index card the top three ideas that they can start to implement immediately into their everyday work.

Ask them to then find partners that are not sitting at their table and discuss what they have written, where it can be used, and how they will implement it. (If their partner offers a good suggestion, this can be added to their own card also.)

Do the same at the end of the day.

Do the same each day if it is a multiple-day workshop.

Newspaper Headline

A simple yet effective review to be done at the end of the day of a long programme.

Provide small teams with the material so they can create a front page of a newspaper onto flip chart paper. The page should reflect their major learnings from the programme. These are suggested materials:

- two newspapers
- one magazine
- scissors
- Pritt Stick
- felt-tip pens

Give them thirty minutes to prepare their chart.

Postcards Home

I will often use this technique to help learners determine their own action plans and remind themselves a month or so afterwards.

Here's how it works:

Ask learners to write down two major action points onto a piece of flip chart paper in large writing. Allow them to specify the "what" and the "when" as well.

Invite each person to the front to describe their action plans to the rest of the group, and at the end take a digital photograph of them standing beside their flip chart sheet.

A month or so later send these photographs to Jessops or someone else and develop them onto a postcard (costs pence for this). Then post them to each delegate as a gentle reminder.

Certificate Ceremony

I'm sure it is not new for you to hand out certificates of participation at the end of the workshop or post these to learners after the event.

Why not make a fun, motivating, celebratory ceremony out of handing out certificates?

Prepare learner certificates prior to the end of the workshop.

Prepare some celebratory music ("We are the Champions" - Queen, "Simply the Best" - Tina Turner, "Holiday" - Madonna).

Let learners know you want to thank them for their contributions during the event and that you want to hand out the certificates.

You will do this in no particular order but would like the rest of the group to show their appreciation for each learner's contributions during the workshop with a warm round of applause and cheers.

Play your music loud and make it a real celebration as you call out and thank each learner.

How to transfer learning to the job

We all know that it's imperative to help the learner transfer the learning back to the job in hand, and here's a great way to do this.

Set up a class blog using blogger, WordPress, or your company's website.

Give each learner email access to post entries to the blog.

Ask them to reflect on their learning and to post a blog entry each week relating to their reflections, how they've used the learning, good news stories.

Allow the other learners to comment on each post, and within a few weeks' you'll have a vastly rich resource of information and ideas to help learners transfer the learning to the workplace, plus a nifty level 3 evaluation piece.

You may need to jog their memory to write their post. Don't ask them for *War and Peace*. A micro blog might work better and make it very easy for them to post blog entries.

Delivering Training with Webinars and Skype

Why we have to be good at this

In January 2007 I spoke at a sales conference in Iran and I was away for just over a week. Nothing unusual in that, apart from Iran which surprises many people. No, the unusual aspect was how I spoke with my family in the evening. Video Skype using a basic laptop with microphone and the hotel's WiFi connection.

Yes, it was grainy, the image shuddered occasionally and was prone to cutting off altogether, but it was an experience to savour and a welcome to the new world of human communication.

Nowadays we have speedy broadband, refined software, and high-definition reaching for the stars, and businesses are beginning to use video capability to talk to suppliers and customers. It's the customer use that excites me; being able to reach out to your customer with the convenience that the Internet gives you is a true evolution in how we communicate. As we improve, more and more customer service people, salespeople will communicate direct to their customers via video.

Are we good at it? Yes and no. Some take to it better than others; some hide away from it. The purpose of this piece is to show you how. It's evolved from extensive research with video-based salespeople and best practices from around the globe, and it will accelerate your learning and skill development so you can immediately give your customer a masterful experience.

Skype, Citrix, FaceTime, Webex...all synonymous with face-to-face communications using the Internet and a device. If you use any of these to do your business, then read on.

The Nine Secrets to being convincing and credible on video

Prolonged eye contact

Exhaustive studies have been carried out over the last century on the impact of eye contact. Eyes are the windows to the soul, and without a connection, there can be no trust. Try talking with someone who stubbornly refuses to remove their sunglasses. There's just no connection; something is missing; trust is not there.

The same goes for video technology. You just have to do the same but more. More prolonged eye contact is needed, which in real life face-to-face, would be construed as staring. And you mustn't look at the customer's eyes; you need to look into the camera.

This is actually harder to do than it seems, especially if the camera is situated towards the top or even on top of the monitor. The instinct is to look at the customer's eyes and face, but do this and they'll see you looking down at them. The answer is to look into the camera and imagine that the customer is behind it. Look straight into the camera and the customer will see that you are giving them eye contact. Occasionally glance or learn to have a sharper peripheral vision so that whilst you're staring into the camera, you can keep an eye on your customer's body language and facial expressions as you engage, but do this with peripheral vision.

A little trick here is to ensure you put your image in a window at the bottom of the screen. That way you know how you are appearing to the customer.

Use more gestures

But keep your hands away from your face. More on the face thing shortly, but if you have your whole top half of your body in the frame, then gestures work as the extra movement creates engagement. Have you ever watched a series of TVs in a showroom? Your gaze is drawn to the screen that is moving, not the blank ones. This is why TV and video are so much more engaging. We are drawn to movement.

Likewise in a video, your gestures create this same effect and bring you closer to your customer.

Don't overdo it and turn into a human windmill. Ensure they are all meaningful and are used to illustrate what you are saying.

Don't hand to mouth

Hand to face is a total negative. Research in body language shows clearly that hand to mouth movements are generally negative, and the hand placed at many points on the head construe adverse readings. Here're some examples of hand-to-face body language and its meaning.

People who want to consciously hide their conversation

Critical Evaluation

"The Thinker"

"Let me Consider"

Difficulty in concluding

Hot under the collar

I know it all

"Well I don't know"

"I can't see it"

Resonant voice

I was trained in hypnotism way back in the '90s as part of my NLP training. Apart from using some of the techniques in my sales training programmes, I rarely use it, but one of the techniques has stayed with me.

A resonant voice.

This has been known in TV circles for decades, and TV presenters, particularly journalists, news readers, learn to develop a more resonant voice. I'm not talking a deep voice, just more resonant.

It appeals to people more, provides credibility, and an aura of knowledge and expertise results. On our workshops and in the MP3s, we provide you with some voice exercises that'll give you a more resonant voice.

Have an expressive face

A deadpan look is for poker players who wish to reveal no emotions. On a side issue, I'll show you shortly how you can read even a poker player's face. But in the meantime, practice your expressions. It's down to movement as before, but also it humanises your video image. The customer needs to know you are real albeit separated by hundreds if not thousands of miles.

Smile more; laugh if the occasion arises; match what the customer is saying with your expression as a sign of listening. For example, if your customer is answering your question about how they might cope in the event of a family tragedy (if you're advising the need for life assurance), the 'if' in their answer is maudling, then show it in your face.

Some people naturally do this; women especially are good at it. If you're not a natural, then you need to develop more expressions.

The little video in the bottom of the screen showing how you come over, is a valuable reminder of this technique. Placing a small hand-held mirror below the screen can also be a useful prompt.

Speak fluently

I was watching a rerun of *Carry on Camping* this weekend, and the voices were very fluent, rather too BBC for my liking. But in that era speaking like a Lord or Lady was the done thing.

Thankfully nowadays, we've moved on, but it still requires that you speak clearly and succinctly so the customer can hear you clearly. Although it's plain to see why, the effect is accentuated by the use of microphones and speakers which don't always mirror the human voice. On the MP3s you'll find some exercises that you can do to become more fluent in your words and remove sibilance – the scourge of the S's.

Pace comes into fluency. Too fast and people may not keep up with you talking, and to a natural slow talker, a pacey salesperson comes across as pushy. Now we don't want that. Try to match your customer's voice pace. But whatever you do, don't talk too slowly compared to them as you will come over as rather lacking in intelligence.

Intonation

Often called Pigeon Toes in call centre circles. Or pitch and tone to you and I.

This links in from the last secret of fluency. It's now down to your tone of voice. Varied is good; monotone is out.

This is something telephone salespeople have been working on since the invention of the phone.

Again, we have some exercises on the MP3s for you to develop your tone.

Face movement

Not to be confused with facial expressions, this one is about moving your head to create a bond with the customer. Let me explain why, then how.

In real-life, face-to-face exchanges, we see three dimensions; we see all of the face, head, and body. At the moment most video is two-dimensional, although changing to 3D rapidly, but I just can't get used to wearing those silly glasses.

To attempt to emulate the 3D experience moving your head around occasionally can show the whole picture to your customer. So move your head to show a profile; tilt your head in an empathic gesture (dogs do this have you noticed), and nod to show agreement with the customer. As before don't overdo this technique. Be real.

Positivity

It's a little "happy clappy", but it shows clearly that those with a positive outlook give a better experience to a customer over video. A glum individual with little or no emotion going through their paces inspires few people.

A positive attitude, looking on the bright side, cheery demeanour all inspire the customer to connect with you in the shortest possible time. And we all know that it takes seconds for a first impression to be formed.

Microexpressions

Our TV is only six years old, but the kids reckon it's ancient. "Belongs in a museum, Dad." Now I'm not going to change the set until it packs up on us. That's the way I am, but the children kept badgering me to look at the new breed of flat-screen high-definition 3D tellies.

Whilst in Currys, buying some equipment for my computer, I happened across their huge range of new TVs. Euan was with me, so we thought we'd have a look. And it blew me away. Screen after screen all paraded along the wall in their fifty-inch-plus glory. A wonderful site, and I was soon fixated on one demo TV, which cleverly showed a split screen. Glued I was.

One-half was old-fashioned TV, like ours at home, showing all the graininess of a crispbread. The other half was HD at its finest. I could even see a bead of sweat on the actor's face and the blushing of his cheeks. I read somewhere that the new breed of TVs are making actors go back to drama school as they have to relearn how to use all the expressions of their faces when acting, rather than the obvious forms of body language. The camera is getting closer and picks out every minute detail, and the actors have to prepare for this.

Back to video-based salespeople. How good are we at using our faces when communicating? The face can give away all sorts of clues to how we're feeling and what's on our mind. Not only can we communicate clearly and congruently if we're aware of the expressions we give, but we can also learn to read the customer's face more in order to move the sales process along to a conclusion.

Now the good news is there is plenty of research into expressions or microexpressions. One of my favourite authors and researchers is Professor Paul Ekman, a psychology expert at the University of California, and his book *Unmasking the Face* is a seminal publication.

Microexpressions are fleeting, involuntary facial expressions that flash on the human face the instant an emotion is felt. The brevity with which they appear on the face differentiates them from longer, voluntary expressions known as macroexpressions.

Microexpressions are often concealed so rapidly that they are nearly imperceptible to the untrained eye, unlike body language and macroexpressions which can be masked.

There are seven known microexpressions, and these can be recognised from humans as early as four years of age, and they are known to cross racial divides and even been tested in monkeys.

Before we train you on recognising the seven microexpressions, let's get practical. You're speaking with your customer on HD-quality video link and you ask them how it all sounds so far. Your customer will respond positively in words, but how many of you instinctively develop a feeling of unease because you suspect not all is in order.

As soon as your customer feels an emotion, within a half second the microexpression reveals:

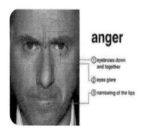

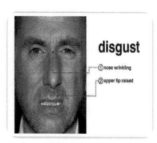

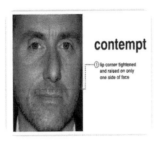

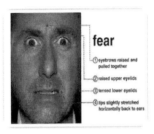

Naturally there are subsets and extremes of these emotions, but the facial microexpressions can be seen clearly for each one.

How to learn Microexpressions

I'm going to show you a picture of them all, an aid memoire, but to learn them I'd like to ask you to download an app for your iPhone or Android phone called Micro Expressions Training, retails at £2.49, not a lot of money to spend on your self-development.

Work through the app. It's very good and will teach you to recognise the split-second microexpression.

Here's a YouTube video to watch. It's a TED Talk – How Body Language and Micro Expressions Predict Success – Patryk & Kasia Wezowski.

http://youtu.be/CWry8xRTwpo

Next try this free test below, or visit the Centre for Body Language for more information on microexpressions in business settings. Again, highly recommended.

http://www.centerforbodylanguage.com/micro-expressions-test

In my experience, the underlying secret is to trust the gut. Trust in your intuition to recognise a microexpression. In real life you can't ask your customer to repeat, unlike the iPod App, so adopt this sequence when learning to read microexpressions:

A final thought is to be aware of your own, but that's another story. And did we upgrade our TV? Boy, of course, we did, to HD glory, and I love watching actor's faces, especially their microexpressions on HD. The best programme to see them is *Downton Abbey*. Have a look yourself.

Voice exercises

The following exercise should be done regularly in order to gain the benefits.

Resonance

As we chatted about earlier, a resonant voice gives you depth and authority alongside a richer voice. It ticks all the boxes of the modern professional expert who wishes to gain credibility quickly. Here's how to develop a resonant voice.

5. Stand or sit but hold your posture well.
1. Choose a note to hum.
2. Next, hum it for an entire breath.
3. Go low with your humming.
4. Feel the vibration in your chest. Learn to recognise the signs of a resonant voice.
5. Repeat.

Clarity and mouth control

Useful for fluency and expressions

1. Stand or sit but hold your posture well.
2. Say a letter out loud as clear as you can, for about ten seconds or your breath runs out.
3. Move your whole mouth and accentuate your cheek muscles.
4. Now do the rest of the alphabet in the same manner.
5. Repeat the alphabet.

Quick clarity

This is a quick exercise to do when you haven't much time.

1. Say the letters QEQR.
2. Move your whole mouth and accentuate your cheek muscles.

Developing intonation

1. If you have children, read a character book and put on some accents.
2. If you don't have children, grab a company brochure and read it as though you were talking to a child. Make it interesting.

How to Develop Video for Trainers

Why should I create video?

Before I start showing you how to create great video, let me share with you why you ought to be doing this.

Firstly I believe that all trainers, be they corporate or self-employed, should be technically capable of using the Internet to aid learning and development. I'm not saying you need to be a coder or flash programmer, but you do need to be able to find your way around web-based applications and software and have a solid appreciation of the cloud and learning management systems.

This leads onto video. Video is not new. Many of us use DVDs in our courses, YouTube clips, and online video to present ideas and concepts. But how many of us actually create video and use these clips in our courses or in our blended learning delivery?

Learners consume video every day. The ubiquitous use of smartphones and tablets mean that everyone has the capability to devour video. People now prefer to watch a video rather than read a web page, YouTube is the second most popular search engine, after Google, and is particularly popular with the Generation Y. And video can paint a thousand words.

More importantly, video can capture a presentation and be consumed by thousands of people simultaneously. Can be paused, rewound, replayed. Can you do that with a live trainer?

Video is great for eLearning, can be delivered via your LMS, is engaging, and expected by the tech-savvy learner. If we don't provide video, we're falling behind the curve.

Let's take a look at how. You'll be pleasantly surprised how easily it can be learnt.

How do I Create Video?

There are essentially two ways of creating video. Outsourcing the whole project to a dedicated production firm or DIY – do it yourself. Outsourcing is where most firms go, but this option is hugely expensive and will only allow you to produce limited footage, but the output is always first-class.

DIY is less expensive and gives you far more control. There are three ways you can do this. Equip a studio with all the equipment you need, use your smartphone, or use your laptop or PC webcam.

Smartphones

Your smartphone will produce decent video which can be edited using software to produce a reasonable final result. Do get yourself some sort of tripod. For a couple of pounds you can buy a tripod that's specifically designed for smartphones. I picked one up this year from eBay and use it for learners to record their own videos in my courses. The tripod stops the jerkiness that will occur without.

Smartphones can be used "selfie" style to record you talking about your topic on location if you wish. I'm often seen walking my dogs self-recording myself sharing a selling tip or idea. It adds realism to the footage, integrity that studio video doesn't have. The major downfall is sound. It's just second rate. You can buy lavaliere microphones for £50 that solve the problem and give your video professional sound. But these are fiddly and remove the portability advantage of the phone.

The other problem is transferring the video onto your PC or laptop for editing. Many smartphones upload videos to cloud storage, and since video sizes are enormous, this process can be very cumbersome. It's best to tether your smartphone to your PC and transfer the footage by cable.

Webcams

These come installed in tablets, laptops, and can be purchased for a few pounds for PCs. They produce good-quality footage and are easily edited because the files reside on your PC after recording. But the outputs just look like webcam videos. People don't look at the camera when they record themselves, preferring to look at the screen, and the output looks stilted, just a trainer talking to the computer.

Backgrounds generally are poor, maybe a bookshelf or a blank wall.

You can record your Skype output easily enough. For £20 you can buy software that will capture your Skype video conversation with someone and output it as a movie file.

I've done this very successfully when interviewing experts or SMEs. Recently I interviewed on Skype, for an hour, the UK's most successful protection salesperson. I used the software to capture the interview and created a series of clips which had both of our images side by side. The audio was okay, and it had a sense of excitement and edginess which made it very engaging.

The Studio

If you want to be able to produce a wide variety of videos, then you really want to invest in a studio with the capability to record video at will. Later I'll show you six types of video which will add variety to the mix and you can only do all of these if you have a fully kitted out studio.

Ideally your studio should be large enough to house all the kit, should have the ability to control outside lighting, and should have an element of sound proofing as well. Corporate trainers will be thinking of a spare room. Self-employed cousins will be thinking of a spare bedroom, garage, or study.

Depending on your budget, you can sound-proof the walls with carpets or specialised wall coverings and buy blackout blinds to obscure all outside lighting. Or you can just close the windows and ask everyone nearby to keep quiet.

You do need a minimum of equipment to be able to produce video, and here's your shopping list in no particular order:

• A giant whiteboard to produce whiteboard-style videos

• A green screen background to produce Chroma Key or green screen video

• A camera. Spend well here. Opt for a prosumer model, but most modern camcorders will produce really good HD video. Make sure it records to an SD card so you can conveniently transfer the final footage to the PC. Don't use the on-camera editing tools; use software on your PC.

• Tripods for the camera

• Autocue device such as a tablet. You position this using a gadget that attaches itself to the tripod so the autocue is just below camera level. Autocues are useful if you haven't memorised the presentation or talk that you're videoing.

• Lavaliere microphones wirelessly connected to your camera. Sound taken from the camera is second-rate. Your learners will forgive you for second-rate footage but will be less forgiving with lousy sound. You can buy a directional external microphone that sits on top of the camera, but a lapel microphone allows you to move around and still pick up excellent sound.

• Lighting. This is the most important aspect in creating truly professional video. As a minimum you'll need two or three hard "barn door"-style lights that can illuminate your green screen and whiteboard plus softer lighting to illuminate your subject's face and body. Google lighting and you'll find dozens of companies that'll advise you. I spent around £300 on lighting.

• Editing software for your PC. These are not expensive, around £100. Don't rely on your PC's free offering. These don't have the features you need. More on this later.

• A very powerful PC that can cope with the demands video rendering puts on the CPU, memory and hard-disk size.

What kind of videos should I create?

I'm going to share with you six varieties of video that you can produce in your studio. Remember, variety is key to learner engagement.

Expert Interviews

Everyone likes an expert and you can very easily interview an expert and record the footage. I mentioned using Skype earlier, but an alternative is to studio record the interview. You can fix up the camera with a directional microphone and just interview your expert with both of you in front of the camera.

A more engaging way is to video your head asking the questions and then switch the camera and video your expert's head providing the answers to the questions. Ensure you position the camera so it stays to the left or right of the eye line of the two people talking, giving the impression of a seamless interview.

With your editing software you can cut the clips and sequence them in the correct order.

Green Screen

My favourite and very professional. I'm sure you've seen these. A trainer appears to the left of the video screen with an ever-changing background. Backgrounds can be movie clips, photos, descriptive words, or animations, and these all add to the message and provide a visual aid to the learner.

Essentially you create a green backdrop to the trainer speaking to the camera. Cover the back wall with a green cloth or buy a stand that'll allow you to drape a green cloth behind you. When you edit the clip on your PC, you remove the green image, which makes the clip transparent. You then add your new background to suit. Render the whole thing to a finished video and you have green screen video.

Whiteboard video

Here you present to the camera using the whiteboard behind you to illustrate your topic. Very engaging and can be used to present complex topics in the same way as you would present in the classroom.

It's best if the whiteboard occupies the whole video screen to give the impression of a whiteboard studio and the trainer stands to one side, not the middle. There's a rule of thirds in video, and the presenter should occupy the left or right side of the picture.

Use a lavaliere or lapel microphone so that sound is picked up even when the trainer has her back to the camera.

PowerPoint video

Very similar, but you use a TV to your side with a PowerPoint presentation. The downfall is that you need to cart a TV into the studio. I find it a whole lot easier and more engaging to put the PowerPoint presentation as the background on a green screen video.

However, if you're bringing in other trainers to be recorded, many are only comfortable if they can use their PowerPoint deck as part of their presentation, and that's totally fine if it helps them present well.

Cartoons and animations

These are fun to produce and even more engaging to watch. You can present something complex in a cartoon storyline and your learners will love it.

Many think you need to be a cartoonist or a flash programmer to encode cartoon videos, but you don't. You do need software, but you only need to spend around £75 to buy software capable of having moving cartoon characters, backgrounds, and words whizzing around the screen. Add a music track and you have a very appealing piece of video.

PowerPoint will do this for you if you know about animation movements and rendering a deck to video.

I particularly like the hand-drawn videos you see on YouTube. These involve a hand mysteriously drawing and writing words narrated in the background or left with music for the learner to read. Again, you can buy inexpensive software to do this for you.

Prezi videos

A Prezi presentation narrated and captured to video can be an extremely attractive way of sharing information with learners.

Software is needed to screen capture and to turn the finished result into video. Set up the pathways in your Prezi and literally present it on the computer talking to the microphone as you would an audience.

The final result is very effective.

How do I edit the video?

As I mentioned earlier, you need to purchase software to render the video and take an online class on how to use it well. Many blemishes can be cleaned up with the software; bad sounds and noises can be removed. You can increase the volume, cut sections out, tidy up the beginning and end, add music for the introduction.

You can't create green screen video without software. Here you add backgrounds of your choosing to spice up the final edit.

The final role of the software is to render the finished item into a file type that can be viewed by the learner. There are a huge variety of file types to use. High-definition, wide-screen, these are all choices. You can also shrink the file size, which is the honourable thing to do if your learner is going to stream the video over the Internet.

Don't under estimate the PC you need. Video rendering software is power and resource hungry. You need a massively fast processor, huge memory, and an enormous hard-drive. A dedicated PC for video rendering is a must. You can't do it on a sub-powered PC or laptop.

How does my learner view the video?

Gone are the days of creating DVDs or cassettes for the learner to view your videos. That's so last century. Nowadays your learner will want to stream the video over the Internet. They will want to use their phone or tablet to watch the clips you produce, or a laptop. This all depends on your IT setup in your company.

As a minimum you'll want somewhere to store your videos in the cloud. You may wish to store them on the company's servers and provide links so your learners can stream them over the intranet.

If you have a learning management system, links can be provided to learners through this medium.

YouTube is a popular cloud storage, but it's very public. You could open an account with Vimeo, which allows unlimited storage and very powerful playback features, and you can password protect them or only allow people with a link to see them.

Have a look at my YouTube Channel – paularcher.tv – you can see how my videos have evolved over the last six years. The earlier ones are horrendous looking at them now, but this serves to illustrate the learning curve I've been on over the last few years.

YouTube and Vimeo give you code that you can put onto your website or blog so that people can view the videos from there, that way you can provide other media such as handouts or PDF documents to read or download to accompany the video.

Summary

This has been a whistle-stop tour of how to create videos for the modern training professional. You don't need an enormous budget, just some creativity some tech awareness and the motivation to want to learn and get better with time.

My advice is just to start and keep evolving. You'll make mistakes but get better and better. I did.

The future of learning and development will move to a web-based, video-based environment so we might as well get good at it now.

Flipping the Classroom – Online Learning

Why Flip the Classroom?

Let me share an analogy of where learning is going, and then I'll give you a roadmap to help you get there.

Let me take you to the music and film industry, which has been well-documented but offers a scary parallel to how we should be taking our learning in the near future.

I'm listening to Blur's "Parklife" right now. Released in 1994, straight to number one—the only place you could buy the album was from a shop, and the CD retailed at £16.99. MTV would show a video and *Top of the Pops* was still on Thursday evening, but you had to tune in at exactly the time the band was playing. Live shows were rare, with an official band tour and only a handful of major festivals. The band made money from record sales.

Twenty years later – 2014 - Arctic Monkeys release their album – *AM*. Available as a download for £6.99 or free streaming on Spotify. Available as an MP3, CD, vinyl. YouTube has free videos of the band that you can access anytime from any device of your choice – smartphone, tablet, laptop, PC, Web TV, for free. Facebook pages, Twitter feeds furnish information about the band. The band plays numerous festivals around the UK. Live is the "big draw" for bands now, far outstripping music sales.

Twenty years has completely changed the music industry. The film and TV sector is also changing rapidly. I was speaking to some young people recently who don't have traditional TV anymore. They use Netflix to watch programmes when they want to and spend an hour a day on YouTube watching quality content—when they want to, not when the broadcasters want us to. The BBC is on a downward spiral. We're only seeing the embryo of their collapse. Sorry, Auntie Beeb, but the modern age is making you no longer fit for purpose.

So where does this lead the learning professionals who are under even more pressure to provide continuous learning to our staff, accelerated with new initiatives – RDR, MMR – and all those currently in the melting pot?

Let me continue the parallel with the music industry and then we'll do some planning.

The State of Learning – 2014

First back to 2004 – learning in financial services corporations. One size fits all, classroom only, very little eLearning. Books and workbooks available. Trainers fluent at delivering face-to-face and coaching. Training design often relates to PowerPoint. Little choice for learners.

In ten years where are we?

2014: Much learning still delivered to learners or provided along pathways to ensure compliance. Classroom still dominates in many firms. Managers call out for more classroom as the quality and value of web-based delivery is not inspiring them. Training pros are good at classroom delivery; some are embracing interactive techniques from the Trainer's Toolbox, some with pressure of time are still throwing a PowerPoint upfront and talking the content through. Easy to create, easy to get approved by compliance.

Learning management systems (LMS) have pretty much landed. eLearning quality varies enormously – internal design staff are complemented by outside contractors and are producing plenty of content that is then made available on the LMS.

Much of it is delivering content or information and has an uncanny resemblance to PowerPoint, which is our point of reference. We're still pushing content at our learners, trying to maintain control of what they learn. Remember the music industry? We like to dip in and listen to our tunes when we want to and use any device we might have to hand.

Webex, ReadyGo, and GotoTraining are being used by early adopters. Once IT firewall restrictions are lifted, this allows us to deliver learning from a distance. Again, quality varies enormously. Some are using interactive techniques; some are merely talking through PowerPoint decks. PowerPoint is reaching the end of its useful life, but we're still hanging on in there.

We're aware of blended learning and are experimenting, but we all have an old reference point. The same thing happened in the music industry. I remember when the big record companies, fearful of their gravy chain coming to an end, tried to stop us from downloading music, sued Napster, then attached the dreaded tags to music so we couldn't play it on more than one device. They tried to control us and we rebelled. And their profits slumped. Now the big money is in live shows; music is a commodity that sells live tickets.

A Self-Perpetuating eLearning Cycle

Each weekend I have a number of jobs to do. Cutting the grass, bringing in a week's worth of logs, checking the oil levels, cutting the hedge. Now my wife knows roughly how long the jobs take from years of watching me and I've trimmed the time down dramatically compared to when I first started. You get into a rhythm, don't you, which speeds up the process.

The same goes for eLearning and corporate designers using their Adobe Captivate and Lectoras.

Developers are tasked with producing this learning, and that learning and the "to do" list gets bigger. They are under time pressure so produce work that is quick, making the most of templates they've already created, shortcuts, reusing pictures and assets, copy and pasting. The result is they can push out lots of eLearning to please the business.

Then the business understands the time it takes and builds its future demands, project timescales and budgets around this. Now the developers don't have time to produce great content, and thus dull elearning results…and lots of it.

And the cycle continues.

The State of Learning – 2024

The next ten years for us learning professionals follow the same path. Let us try to shed what the past offered and rethink the whole learning episode. Here's 2024.

2024 – On-demand learning through a variety of channels. Online, curated content, automated delivery, video, lectures on demand via video, online real delivery using video/holograms of learners. LMS control and create records, but we let our learners explore and learn in their time, trusting them to do it.

Content is now available on phones, watches, Google Glasses, and tablets predominate everywhere. Always on access to forums, social media platforms allow learners to chat and share, video-based, for discussion. Learning professionals facilitate this.

Corporate trainers are multi-skilled in analysing, designing, and developing online learning using a wide variety of software methods and tailoring it to their customers. Web-based learning engages, absorbs, and interacts with learners. It's exciting, gamified, challenging. It has to be since the competition is fierce and free. Learning on any topic or technique is freely available on the web, and the learners that we're working with have been weaned on this, so we had better compare favourably.

Just enough, just in time, and just for me.

Live, face-to-face, is the money spinner. Live events can command large audiences. Those learning professionals who can do this become highly paid. They deliver their live events using web video or for real to select audiences.

Learning should be – just enough, just in time, and just for me – and by 2024 if we're not doing this, we will wither on the vine.

Ten Steps for the Ten-year Plan

Change your methodology

Remove the influence that compliance has on this. Most are not learning professionals; push back. Simplify the process to create good learning, and empower non-L&D people to do this.

Bring in "Super Trainers"

World War I is totally in focus this year, being 100 years since hostilities began. The Germans almost won it using StormTroopers or Sturmtruppen. These specially trained soldiers used advanced techniques to spearhead the advance. Super Trainers are highly trained in analysing needs and determining performance and learning objectives and can work with all business heads to decide solutions, many of which are non-training.

They have sound instructional design skills.

They then have the capability of designing learning solutions, flipping the classroom completely on its head, using a variety of methods. They have teams who can design; some can do this themselves also. When it comes to delivery, they're the Robbie Williams of their generation, and they're very well-paid, on par with business heads.

All learning professionals need to develop an "influencing sphere" in the business. The sphere will be their customers and must include senior leaders across the piste. This sphere needs to extend beyond customers, IT, compliance, risk. The ability to influence and persuade becomes a requisite skill, and we need to adopt various powers to do so. Ultimately positional, expert, and personal powers.

Start mastering the technology available.

I mean mastering its capabilities, not just using 10% of the features, but don't let technology rule. Remember, it's learning, not technology, that matters.

Don't rely on one "all in one" software solution. Use a suite of software to perform a variety of tasks. Continue to digest new programmes and apps constantly being developed.

Let go of control

Learn to work the LMS, not let the LMS work you. Make your LMS easy to use with the ability of learners to drop in when they want to consume learning.

Corporate learning and development teams often have large and diverse audiences of customers to cater for along with the larger projects with scrumptiously big budgets.

Catering for everyone can be achieved by adopting the Amazon.com model – the long tail. See the appendix for a description of the long tail and how this relates to learning and development.

The strategy to aim for is a learning content management system – an LCMS. This is an online repository of every asset ever created or bought by L&D which can be searched easily by anyone in the organisation, not just L&D people. The LCMS can form the basis of the "on demand" material with the LMS itself and can be used by anyone designing a learning programme, without having to reinvent the wheel.

Naturally bespoking can occur to design a tailored solution, but often this luxury of time is not there in a busy corporate L&D team, so using pre-created assets can save a lot of time.

We need to start curating the content now and tagging every item properly. The tag is hidden within the file, often in properties, and is used for the searching.

Just enough

Make the learning on demand and let the learner choose what they want to do. Don't deliver content, let them consume it. Concentrate your efforts on how to do their job better, and align all learning closely to the job. This helps with the 70% of the 10:20:70 model.

Concentrate on achieving the business objectives set when the learning need was originally revealed. Look for all non-training solutions as well as training solutions. Achieve the objectives with the least resources - that's good business.

Think mobile

BYODs, tablets, smartphones, as learners will consume learning on these devices, anywhere and on demand.

Just in time

Be nimble in design and delivery. Be prepared to change and adapt it. Adopt rapid eLearning authoring packages to produce 75% of your learning, and do it quickly, just in time. You don't need a flash coder or programmer to use rapid eLearning, just familiarity with PowerPoint. The next 20% of your learning can be hybrid. In other words, combining rapid eLearning with custom development, and the final 5% can be totally customized using expensive resources or outsourced.

Supplement rapid eLearning with custom development

Use flash assets and objects created elsewhere and incorporate into your rapid authoring tool.

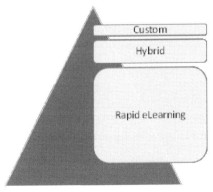

Adopt the four stages of learning design

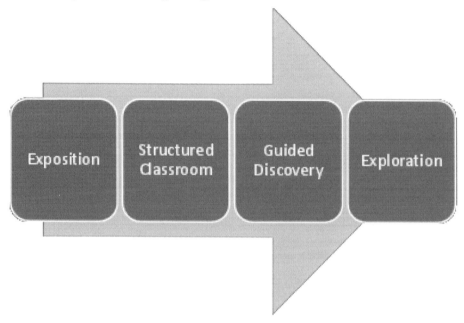

- Exposition is material which you simply expose the learner to. You make it available, typically on an LMS, and the learner dips into it as and when they please. Pre-recorded materials – multimedia – video, audio, written material…the list goes on. Record everything and make it available for exposition.

- Structured classroom or instructor-led training usually to a group and highly structured, often with interaction and engagement. The what and the how is often covered in this manner. This can be eLearning, live web classroom, or a physical classroom.

- Guided discovery is more simulation-based exercises to discover things, simulations to practice techniques and experience the consequences of getting it wrong. Online games and simulators, coaching. This is where the why and when is covered.

- Exploration is totally learner-centred and informal. Using Wikis, blogging, social media…the learner explores to find the information and ideas they're looking for.

Just for me

Maximize variety and differing learning styles. Use a blended approach. Here are some suggestions:

- Captivate-style eLearning streams containing the full VARK learning styles. Use more advanced software, such as ZebraZapps, create gamified learning experiences, buy plugins and other assets for a matter of dollars to insert. Don't reinvent the wheel.

Gamification is using elements of video games and putting them into serious business learning activities. Don't just reinvent a PowerPoint deck into flash software.

- Live workshops using GoTo, Webex but engaging the audience and involving them with breakouts, whiteboards, quizzes, activities broken down into hour-or-less chunks – not PowerPoint and a narrator. Record them to create an asset for learners to go back to. Firewalls need dropping, but that's an easy solution.

- Video – can be used in a variety of ways. An expert or speaker presenting to camera in a lit room with whiteboard, a live recording of a presenter with an audience, SMEs presenting and demonstrating skills, an interview with two or more people, a live recording of something happening like a client interview, a directed piece of video to explain and demonstrate something. The list goes on. A great book to reference if you want to know how is *Rapid Video Development for Trainers: How to Create Learning Videos Fast and Affordably* by Jonathan Halls.

- Blogs, Wikis containing information to digest – text, videos, podcasts – plus the ability of the user to generate content.

- Use animation and motion-graphic software to produce learning events that engage. Toon Boom Animate, PowToon, SWiSHmax. Place these in your learning authoring packages for that professional high-end touch.

- Prezi canvasses either rendered into a video or as HTML planted in your LMS for learners to pick and choose where to go. A wonderful example of this comes from a travel insurance client who used a Prezi containing hundreds of medical conditions with descriptions based around a human body. Click and zoom, it really engaged the learner.

- RCA-type hand-drawn animations to explain something and then rendered into a video clip. Use VideoFX, Explandio, videoscribe.co, or GoAnimate.com.

- Interviews with SMEs, face-to-face using sound recording and rendering to a podcast. A series or one-offs. Video could be used here as well.

- SlideShare or recording PowerPoint decks to a video with sound narration. Or created using massive visuals and strong words to allow the learner to read and engage.

- Use Google Moderator to prime your customers before the learning event. This free app allows learners to log on to discuss the learning, submit questions, and hook up before the event. Needs moderating by the trainer but really useful in helping to create a tailored event.

- YouTube Videos. There are millions of these, as we know, and a link from your LMS can take your learner here or take the HTML code and embed it into your LMS. Vimeo also hosts some great content.

- Simulations for software training. Use show and tell as well as imitate.

- eCoaching. Our first traditional piece of learning. Coaching face-to-face or eCoaching using Skype with video. Coaching via the learning professionals or the line managers takes care of the 20% of the 10:20:70 model.

- Skype discussion groups, Google Hangouts. A place where a small group of learners can gather together to debate an issue and run an exercise of collaborative learning.

- Discussion forums for learners to debate their learning, chat to their peers, and get some help with something. Naturally moderated, of course, but don't be afraid to hear what's what. Let go of any fear and let go of delivering training, and let them learn.

- Online quizzes, gameshow events. The gambling industry has this area nailed. Create quiz shows online for learners to attend. Central database of all questions/multi-choice, etc., and design games around this for learners to have fun, spend money, and win money and prizes. Have automation so questions are delivered to learners' inboxes. Keep momentum going.

- Traditional instructor-led classes using the full range of the Trainer's Toolkit. The toolkit comprises dozens of methods of training which allow interaction and engagement.

- Many of these assets can be delivered using a Captivate-style vehicle to run on your LMS or as video clips to stream using Vimeo or the like. It's a case of creating digital content that can be accessed by your learner, just for me, just enough, and just in time.

The Long Tail in L&D

The long tail in retail was first mooted in 2004, and Amazon is famous for illustrating its effect.

Take the book market. Before online retailers like Amazon, the only place you could buy a book was in a store, and they could only physically stock so many books. So they focused on the best sellers, those destined to be bought by the masses. They couldn't cope with the long tail.

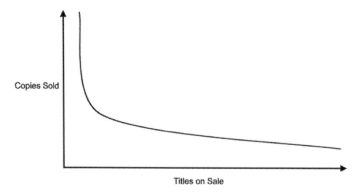

Only when Amazon came on to the market did they start to ramp up their stocks of other books and could you then service the long tail—smaller numbers of people buying more specialised books in smaller numbers. Amazon made this an essential part of their business, and profitable too.

Move this to the world of training and development. We have training to deliver to large audiences and projects to smaller audiences – the long tail. eLearning as a solution can deliver to both sets of audiences, but of course, a larger audience gives you more budget so you can tailor an experience using hybrid and specialised solutions.

But where's the money for the long tail? Here is where we adopt rapid eLearning or utilising our content library of eLearning assets to bring together a programme.

It looks like this:

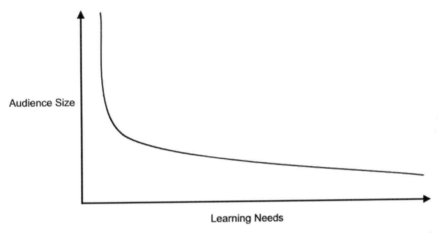

So here is a model to help you cope with the everyday pressurised demands from the business and still provide engaging and results-driven learning solutions.

If Amazon did it, so can we.

How to make your eLearning more engaging

The Holy Grail for many, how to engage your learner more in the eLearning that you produce. Many of my clients yearn after ways to engage; involve more; and spend time, money, and other resources on interactive games, Trivial Pursuit activities, Jeopardy, whizzy things, and animations to engage.

They want to move the continuum from left to right.

But it often doesn't work.

Why?

Simple actually – they spend time on razzing up the "what and how" of their eLearning, and this is not how you engage learners. You see the "what and how" is often information, processes, systems, understanding. And there's not a huge amount you can do here to make it really interactive.

The secret is to spend time on the "why and when" in the form of a simulation. We must learn to mimic their roles, their jobs, so they can experience the learning in their current roles. We need to provide an experience which allows them to have a go, make mistakes, learn.

In the classroom this is often conducted through role play or forum theatre with coaching and feedback. Good role play can make all the difference to learning the job.

In eLearning we can do the same, and when done well, will make the learning more interactive and engaging.

To do this you must take their job they currently do. Cut out a two-hour segment and guide them through a sequence of decisions with the relevant consequences.

For example, I'm currently working on an online programme for mortgage advisers to help them sell more protection assurance. I've taken a two-hour segment from their jobs and have programmed various "moments of truth" which involve the right decision to be made. In the elearning simulation, we have a cartoon image of the mortgage adviser with details of their diary for the afternoon on the screen.

This is remarkably like the job they do, so immediately the attention is gained because the learning is relevant to their jobs and they can see that completing it will make them better at what they do and help them sell more plans towards their targets.

The first decision is a "pre-call" that they need to make to a customer who is calling in tomorrow morning. The call is going well, and they need to outline next what the meeting involves. The eLearning will give them various options, and they need to select the right one.

Now the screen isn't going to say right or wrong…at that time. The decision they make just moves the simulation in a different direction and the consequences of making the wrong decision can change the course of the simulation.

You see, that's the point. They don't have to get it right; they just need to experience making various decisions and the consequences involved. That way they learn. Think back to the major learnings you've had before. I bet they were as a result of making a mistake. It is for most of us.

So spend time and effort on the why and when, and this will ensure your eLearning becomes more interactive and engaging.

Eight Future Trends in Training and Development

November 2012…Tewkesbury, Gloucestershire…flood alert.

It's the two rivers joining that cause the problems here in Tewkesbury, and when both rivers are swollen with rain water, they converge on Tewkesbury and, inch-by-inch, push river water over the banks, across the flood plain, and into the town and people's houses.

Inch-by-inch the water level rises, and there's nothing you can do about it except try and use sandbags or other devices to protect your belongings. The river always wins.

Inch-by-inch the water level rises; it's slow, continuous, and unstoppable.

It's a bit like the future of corporate training and development. The Internet has enveloped many industries already and will, inch-by-inch, take over the remainder. Just observe the music industry, the world of movies, estate agency, electrical gadgets, and books.

The Internet has only lightly touched training and development so far. If you think it's cloaked, you're wrong.

But inch-by-inch it will begin to envelop it over the next few years. Allow me to explore the changes that we can see ahead and how these will affect training and development professionals.

The Internet tsunami – we must apply it. We don't need to teach.

The Internet contains everything you ever need to do anything. How to unblock a drain, understanding the negative correlation in investment portfolios, and ideas for Christmas presents for someone who has it all.

Mobile Internet has only exacerbated this. We can now look up how to trim a rose bush whilst waiting for the number 91 bus. Mobile Internet will dominate as we browse our tablets and smartphones, and with 4G coming along with lightning-fast download speed, this trend will accelerate.

So if we have every piece of information on our phones, why don't we just use this exclusively? Because there is just too much, cluttered with advertising, spam websites, erroneous information, dated data. It's like drowning.

Look carefully, though, and you can see the Internet de-cluttering information and making it easy for us to consume, sometimes for free, but increasingly being charged for. Take the BBC and the Open University, collaborating to show excellent information, knowledge, and techniques from two trustworthy brands – for free.

Or Wikipedia or YouTube – the greatest depository of techniques, strategies, and how-to on earth.

Our role as training and development professionals is to utilise the Internet but focus our attentions on applying the knowledge, using it, making it fit. It's the application of techniques and knowledge which is the key, not regurgitation of knowledge that someone can quite easily look up for themselves. They'll pay us for being able to apply it, not look it up.

This weekend my seventeen-year-old son came home from school moaning that he didn't understand the negative externality of demand and supply. Nor did I, until we played a YouTube video together and I was able to help Lewis apply this theory and give him some examples to bring it to life. My role as a trainer was to find the information and apply it to the question or challenge.

That's how we'll work alongside the Internet. Work with it, not against it.

Training simulators

Continuing this theme of applying knowledge and techniques, we need to mature our use of training simulators. Pilots, train drivers, air traffic controllers use them to hone their skills before practicing further on expensive airplanes or trains. So should we.

If you previously had the word "skills" on your course programmes, e.g., listening skills, sales skills, or meeting skills, then you can only advertise these if you have some sort of training simulation dominating the course programme. You see, to gain a skill in something, you have to learn the techniques and then apply them to your world. For example, learning meeting skills can't be done in a classroom setting in the traditional sense. Instead, learn with PowerPoint how to chair a meeting or the five principles of running a group discussion.

You can get this from the Internet; YouTube will have hundreds of videos on these topics. Instead we need to help our people develop these techniques into skills, and the only way to do this is to help them apply to their world. In other words, how to run a group discussion with the quietest, demotivated team in the building who have been sent to a meeting to be creative and inspiring. It has to be the real world – all hairy and warts – to become a skill.

Our role is to set up this simulation in the first instance and apply the techniques to become a skill.

Many of us do this in a classroom already with role play, or role play on steroids using actors playing the parts of real people. That's a simulator. Or better still, a web-based simulation package. Or even better than that, as a trainer we should evolve into coaches and go with our learner to their workplace and observe and coach them whilst they're running the meeting.

All trainers should be excellent coaches and have the credibility and substance to be able to relate to the real world, to be experts at applying knowledge and techniques. No longer can training departments be filled with career trainers who haven't experienced the real world, but experienced, credible individuals steeped in the ability to apply.

Gamification

Gamification – taken from the burgeoning gaming market.

I was reading the Economist this week, and they stated that the gaming industry is now worth $67 billion, rivalling the movie industry. Games offer excitement, entertainment, challenge, and the ability to win, and it's this gamification that will affect training enormously in the next few years.

In their new book *For the Win*, Werbach and Hunter argued that future communications can be enhanced by gamifying their style. Gamification has now entered the management buzzword directory.

Games have distinct ingredients, and so must our trainings and coachings.

I talk about WIPEing the message.

- W is for win. Can the activity that you create to communicate allow them to win something?

- I is for instant feedback. How can the group players get instant feedback?

- P is for points or badges to signify progress and success, and

- E is for excitement, which tells its own story.

So trainers, sales managers with a message, will want to gamify their offering, particularly with online training.

Low attention spans

I believe we've always tried to squeeze a round peg into a square hole when we run our long two- or three-day programmes. I don't believe people have an attention span big enough, and they never have. But with the advent of the Internet and information at your fingertips, this attention span has shrunk even further.

Now there is no average attention span of an adult. It really depends on them, the subject, state of mind, the weather, etc.

But what is clear is that we can't deliver traditional training in outdated ways. It needs to be short and sharp and delivered in bite-sized portions if we want to maintain attention.

I'm not referring to the method of training delivery. I'm focussing purely on the timing. We can deliver bite-sized face-to-face, on the job, or online via smartphones.

Web delivery

The Internet will encase training and development by making it the place to deliver our training. We've all experienced static webinars; these are improving. The future will be on demand learning via the Internet. People will pay for on-demand learning if it saves them time searching the Internet.

Web delivery in the future will mirror what we are capable of doing face-to-face. That's when video will take over. If we're presenting, then stand. Don't crouch in your seat in front of a webcam. Imitate what you currently do but deliver through the Internet. Get used to presenting in front of a camera, imagining your audience behind the lens.

One client I work with has invested in web delivery for the future. They've converted two rooms into video rooms, kitted them out with the latest video and sound equipment. Their trainers pitch up and deliver their training in the room to an audience on the Internet, not in front of them. Yes, they have a long way to go, since the trainers are pretty much mirroring how they would normally train just in front of a camera. They are adapting to involve the audience more, talking with them rather than at them, running group exercises, and letting the audience do the talking too.

It will come with time.

Applying the learning can be achieved using web delivery. Discussion forums work very well, and in the future we'll all be using video-based discussion forums where best practice is shared and ideas debated.

Webinars are common; they allow the giving of information generally. Yes, you can put your hands up and ask questions, but they're mostly clunky and technology-dependent. Try running a Google+ Hangout immediately afterwards so a few people can discuss how to use the ideas whilst looking each other straight in the eye. That's the capability of the Internet that we'll be using more in the future.

The real future lies in something rather different, though. More on that later. Just imagine *Star Trek's* holodeck.

A tailored suit

The price of clothing, and particularly suits, has plummeted so much that you can buy a suit from the supermarket for £20. Admittedly it's not the best cut in the world – you get what you pay for. It does make the cost of a tailored suit somewhat cheaper though - £200 to £300 is not uncommon, a figure you would pay for a decent suit a few years ago.

A good tailor can reduce your waistline by at least two inches and make you look a stone lighter. And sliding into a tailored, fitted suit is luxury.

In the same way, all training in the future should be tailored. Off-the-shelf-type learning events just don't cut it anymore. You can get the same outcome from the Internet.

Tailored or bespoked training takes more time to develop but can focus exclusively on applying the learning. You can involve other methods, such as web delivery, to supplement if you wish. You can use real examples, actors to bring the application to life, put the learning in the workplace. You can do all sorts of things to ensure it makes a difference.

The future of bespoked training again is the application of the learning using simulators. But off-the-shelf courses will disappear.

In company, on the job

Released from the shackles of off-the-shelf learning programmes or standardised eLearning packages, you can focus your trainings on the job, in the office, on the factory floor. The future will require corporate trainers to own strong shoes as they wander and labour alongside the workforce. Armed with their tablet devices able to access information from the Internet, videos on demand, these highly trained coaches will help people apply the learnings and techniques.

They'll deliver short, sharp sessions, where needed and when required. In fact, the manager of the future will be doing more of this, and we've been preaching this for ages.

Expertise

With the demise of off-the-shelf programmes, stagnant eLearning packages, generalised training, trainers will become more specialised and expert at what they do.

Future trainers will be experts in their field; people will demand this. They will be expert not only at their subjects and skills but in being able to distil the Internet and apply the learnings to people's jobs. People will pay for expertise in the future, not generalists. The Internet will become next year's generalist.

Trainers will be able to apply real-world insights and wisdom, be an asset to complement the Internet, not try to imitate it.

That's the future of training and development.

The last word – the real future

First came MPG1 which compressed audio files, followed by MP2, and then the ubiquitous MP3 that now dominates our music players, swiftly followed by MP4 which has done the same to video clips. The next step will be compressed holographic files which can send your hologram through the Internet to meet with someone else's hologram in a virtual meeting room.

That's maybe five years away, maybe longer to bring the cost down, but that's when the floodwaters will reach their peak, and training and development will be completely cloaked by the Internet. Just wait and see.

The Virtual Classroom – A Case Study

My first foray into the training world was in the early 1990s working for a corporate estate agency. I headed up a team of trainers, and our job was to develop the country's financial adviser population.

No Internet, no Skype, no Google, no PDF files, no smartphones.

Just landlines, photocopiers, expensive car phones, and meeting rooms.

So the vast majority of training delivery involved sending out pre-course photocopied packs of reading matter followed by the ubiquitous face-to-face training course.

Whiz forward twenty years and the training world has changed beyond measure.

Skype, mega-fast broadband, YouTube, MOOCs, and smartphones capable of watching live streaming videos and with more computer power than the desktop PCs I used back in the early 1990s.

These days, corporates won't allow their teams to leave their jobs to attend long classroom training sessions. There's actually no need to do so, and the trainer who embraces this will be the trainer who survives.

Let me share with you how, using a real-life case study to show you the process and impact.

The case study

In early 2013, I was commissioned to run some technical training for a large bank here in the UK. Their 500 staff needed development to be able to pass a series of exams to ensure their compliance with the new regulations.

The brief was simple. Help them to pass the exams by the end of the year, but they're all currently active in the bank and we can't ship them into classrooms for weeks on end.

And that's my point, because twenty years ago that's what we would have done. Created a set of acetates and trained them for weeks on end in a classroom. The cost was incredible, but we had no other way of doing it and achieving success.

But today we have.

So I set about determining how. So let's examine the virtual classroom methods available to us today, and I'll share my thinking as to the ones we used for the project.

But first, the case study in more detail.

The Scene

The bank is a large multinational with thousands of staff around the world. They provide services and products to both consumers and businesses, but the staff requiring the training operate on the retail side.

The 500 or so staff range from very experienced to new graduate recruits. They are a complete mixture of generations and experience. However, the majority are Generation Y.

The main challenge for the bank was to increase the technical knowledge of the individuals to be able to pass the exams, thus ensuring their continued employability and compliance with the regulator.

Additional information

The timeframe was six months from first delivery to taking all the exams.

There were five exams in total, allowing for a month for each exam study period. However, we were up against deadlines that quickly loomed so didn't have too long to plan too laboriously. Decisions had to be made quickly and implemented straightaway. Welcome to the real world.

Staff was widely dispersed across the UK and were all working full-time in branches with plenty of things to do in a busy banking environment. Taking time out was a premium.

Resources available

We had a team of technical trainers capable of delivering the content, who were quite used to running classroom-based courses and were lively in their delivery style.

We had budget to spend. The bank was clearly aware of the cost of classroom courses for the 500 people so were able to provide a reasonable budget to deliver this virtually, or at least, part virtually.

We had budget for equipment, software, and licenses, and we had premises, speedy broadband, and technical expertise.

People and Stakeholders

The main stakeholder in the bank was the training director supported by a team of practitioners – compliance people, training staff, and sales management staff.

Planning phase

Various meetings were held between stakeholders, determining objectives and challenges followed by meetings with the delivery team and myself.

The expectations from the client were actually quite limited. They were used to receiving recorded webinars with trainers talking over PowerPoint slides – typically wordy and detailed. These recordings were made with webinar software such as GoTo or Webex.

Interestingly the staff who were on the receiving end were not too excited about the same delivery but expected it to be so and were "grinning and bearing" it.

We agreed to expand our capability to deliver something exceptional for the client within budget and timescales, to push the needle, so to speak.

Our first step was to examine what was currently available to produce virtual classrooms.

Options considered

eLearning Packages

Traditional eLearning packages were debated. These are off-the-shelf or customised software packages that allow learners to follow a course of study via their PC. They are typically attached to a complex learning management system that monitors and provides reports on staff progress. They are very powerful for auditing and recordkeeping requirements, ideal for a heavily regulated bank.

The bank had one, of course, but didn't have access or budget to use it or create the learning around it. The cost was many hundreds of thousands of pounds and relied totally on the quality of the actual learning modules within the learning system.

Typically these consisted of words on screens, mini tests, the occasional video clip, but rare. The systems tethered the staff to company PCs in company rooms for a period of time whilst they enjoyed their training.

Research with staff had shown that they had anchored their previous experience of the eLearning systems, which placed them in a certain state of mind as they entered the room. We decided to try and change that.

Live Webinars

Liver webinars have enjoyed huge popularity over the last five years. They have become popular because of a perfect storm. Rising fuel prices to prohibit travel; security concerns about travelling on trains, planes, and automobiles; increasingly sophisticated technology; fast broadband; and an economic downturn driving the aim of cutting training costs.

Bad webinars consist of someone talking to an audience using wordy slides to help them remember what to say. Little or no audience interaction, rare use of multimedia.

However, you can deliver them to hundreds of people simultaneously so it fitted the audience, but this mass audience prevented interaction.

Good webinars involve the audience, ask questions, use polls, share whiteboards, involve the tutor's video image, encourage Q&A's, but true interaction requires a smaller audience so more webinars would be needed to deliver the training.

Trainers can deliver webinars via their homes, and staff can view them in their offices or at home. They can be recorded to provide a video clip to be watched at the audience's leisure. This is what they were used to, and the quality of the webinars they viewed was on the lower scale. Although technically very detailed and accurate, this meant a low-engaging delivery.

Teleseminars

Relying totally on the spoken word, these were very popular in the early 'naughties' as a way of delivering information to large audiences. Simply a trainer dials in to a number and talks, and a number of people also dial in and listen. With smaller numbers of listeners, you can take questions from the audience, but with larger numbers this can get quite unmanageable.

With just the spoken voice to rely on, attention spans can be challenged and people often multi-task whilst listening.

Recordings can be made and delivered to the audience's PCs and listened to as podcasts. Podcasts were made famous by Apple and its iPod, hence the name pod and broadcasts, i.e., podcasts. They are recorded audio conversations, teleseminars or pre-recorded studio conversations at the other end of the spectrum.

Learners can load them onto their phones or MP3 players and listen to them at their leisure.

There's very little interaction, and they do rely on the speaker's voice being engaging, and many are not.

Skype Group Meetings

Skype is very well-known and provides the ability to video someone else wherever they are in the world, for free.

Pay a little extra and you can enjoy premium, which gives you the ability to run a Skype video call with to up to eight people. They are live and involve people's faces and expressions, which changes a lot of the dynamic, particularly attention. The speaker can share screens, maybe a PowerPoint slide or their desktop, perhaps a web page.

Everyone can talk and chat to each other, and the screen can show all eight images of the people on the meeting.

These can be recorded as well and made available as a pre-recorded session and delivered as a video.

Google Hangouts

Google+, which is its Facebook, offers a facility where you can hang out with people in your circles. Hanging out allows you to video chat with your colleagues much the same way as a Skype group call.

The hangout comes to life when you link it to your YouTube channel, and then the video output can be viewed live by anyone. Great if you have mass audiences using varying systems, to be able to watch with little inconvenience. For example, someone can be on an iPad, someone else on an Android phone, somebody using a Windows-based laptop. YouTube is ubiquitous so poses no problems.

It's not very private, but you can add passwords if you wish.

Recorded video clips

Video is enjoying a renaissance thanks to the Internet. We're so much more engaged with video now with Facebook, sites such as BBC and Sky full of streaming videos, blogs containing videos, Netflix, LOVEFiLM Instant. The list goes on. We're very familiar with video, and fast broadband speeds, quick mobile Internet speeds make this video easily digested.

Trainers can quite quickly and cheaply record themselves on a video using their phone or a high-end camera or a webcam came built into their laptop or tablet. Just go onto YouTube and you'll see subject experts teaching all sorts of subjects.

You'll see people:

- Talking to their webcam

- Standing up presenting to the camera

- Drawing on a flip chart whilst talking to you

- Using a whiteboard whilst teaching you

- Running a PowerPoint show on a large, flat-screen TV next to them

- Outside on a Cornish hillside teaching you a topic

Quality varies enormously with video, and to some, this doesn't matter – it's the content, the speaker, and the length that really matter. Research shows that the average attention span on a YouTube video is thirty seconds. Some think it's less.

Quality can range from holding your iPhone in front of you whilst activating video recording all the way to studio-quality green screen videos with lapel microphones and studio-quality lighting. It's down to budget and what you want to achieve.

YouTube Videos

Merely searching for an appropriate YouTube video that someone else has created and using this to teach your subject. There are literally millions of videos which can be freely viewed on YouTube. The trouble is finding the right one amongst the haystack.

PowerPoint shows

Create a PowerPoint deck and have it recorded to video, capturing your voice and transitions on the PowerPoint. The ability to record is contained within PowerPoint, or you can use screen capture software to put the whole show onto a video that can be played. PowerPoint can be quite multimedia-based – photos, large text, videos, graphs – and an engaging voice can really make this medium quite compelling.

Video playback

Where do you put the finished videos so that everyone can play them on any medium they choose – laptop, PC, TV, iPad, tablet, iPhone, smartphone, iPod...the number of devices capable of playing videos is enormous, so your video needs to be totally compatible with them all.

So putting a video on your website may not work on an Apple PC or an iPhone but might play on a Windows tablet. There are an enormous number of file types.

YouTube has this cracked as they encode your video that you upload so it can be run on a multitude of devices with little or no problem. This is all free, well, sort of; there's a huge amount of advertising going on with YouTube, and this earns Google billions of dollars.

Besides, it's very tricky to put passwords on YouTube, although this is all changing with private viewing channels and TV shows that you pay for.

So YouTube is a venue for your videos, but there are others. One we like is Vimeo. Pay a few dollars per month and have your own Vimeo where you can store all your videos. No advertising and you can create channels and albums to plop your videos in for easy access and viewing. Vimeo also renders the videos so they are streamed to any device under the sun, and they do it well.

There are many others.

Prezi shows

Prezi has only been live for about two to three years. It's a way of presenting information in a multimedia format and has often been described as an alternative to PowerPoint.

It's very different and very funky. And that's its downfall. The viewer of the prezi can get caught up in all the flashy graphics, colours, words flashing around, 360-degree views on the topic, and constant movement. So much that they don't take in the content.

Prezi is a giant canvass where you place your content anywhere inside and create your own path to display the content. It is nonlinear. PowerPoint is. PowerPoint starts from slide number 1 and continues to the end. Prezi can start anywhere and finish anywhere, and the viewer can take control and view bits on their own.

That sounds fine, but an element of control is needed, some order and structure to presenting information, so, in the same manner as PowerPoint shows, you can run a Prezi presentation, narrate it through your microphone, and turn the whole presentation into a video.

The major benefit is you can display all sorts of content. Many of the places I've already mentioned can be inserted and included in your Prezi, and the whole Prezi template can be viewed as a giant metaphor, like a holding bay for all the other multimedia you have created – whiteboard videos, Skype calls recorded as videos, podcasts, PowerPoint slides, and so on.

Implementation

Decisions were then made on the capability of the team, as much of the delivery was quite technical and did alarm some of the trainers on the team, so a small cohort of experts set about training everyone on some of the technical aspects, such as:

- How to operate Prezi, create a canvas using a template, and populate the Prezi

- How to screen capture to a video clip

- How to open a Vimeo account and upload videos, creating albums, and password protecting

- How to render video using video software, adding words, etc.

- How to upload to YouTube

- How to record a podcast on a computer

- How to video yourself presenting with a whiteboard or flip chart using a basic video camera

- How to capture your voice professionally using a lapel microphone

Once everyone was familiar with the various tools and software, the reticence to do anything differently soon fell away, and the whole team began to explore the options without fear of a lack of technical knowledge. This was, however, still evident in some of the trainers' preferences. Experience shows that the majority of subject expert trainers don't like to do things too differently.

We implemented the following:

- We split the topics into the six separate subjects and set about creating virtual classrooms for each topic.

- We split each topic into four separate virtual classrooms, each lasting approximately two hours. So eight hours of virtual delivery was proposed for each subject.

- The trainer, who had the expertise and experience of bringing the topic to life, was chosen for each subject, and they became the manager and had technical experts on hand to help, i.e., those who were technically minded and knew their Vimeos, from the MP4s and rendering from their uploading.

- We decided to create a corporate Prezi account utilising their desktop version so trainers could create Prezis without Internet access or with slow broadband. Templates were chosen for each virtual classroom to allow for consistency and the visual metaphor carefully chosen.

- Trainers then determined what multimedia they would build into their Prezi to cover the topics in the way they wanted. They went about recording whiteboard and flip chart videos of themselves, presenting short snippets of their usual classroom performance. Video clips of them lasted, on average, five minutes each. Technical help was on hand to record those not comfortable doing so, using lapel microphones to create a rich sound.

- Videos were rendered and cleaned up using Sony Vegas software by the technical team or trainer, if they felt comfortable doing so.

- Other multimedia chosen to present the topics within Prezi included:
  o Photographs (we opened an account with iStockphoto to ensure compliance)
  o Key bullets in a Prezi frame
  o PDF pages to act as a handout within Prezi
  o YouTube videos selected as appropriate and available for general viewing
  o Podcasts
  o Royalty-free music clips to add that extra sparkle
  o Overhead recordings of hands drawing on a blank page illustrating a point
  o PowToon cartoon graphics and flash animation

o   RSA-type animations, hand-drawn whiteboards

The key was to embed within the Prezi template a wide selection of multimedia to suit all the learning styles of the learners, with a heavy bent on visual which heads the league table of learning styles.

Once they were ready, the trainers joined every element of Prezi to a logical and structured path and played the Prezi with their own voice narrating the words, introducing the videos, watching the YouTubes, and so on. This whole process was screen captured into a compressed video clip

The clip, which could last up to forty-five minutes, was rendered and cleaned up, then uploaded to an album within Vimeo, password-protected, and the URL address passed on to the bank that made them available to their learners in their pre-determined order.

Learners followed the virtual classrooms, some watching them on their work PCs, some at home, and some on the train on the way to work using the Vimeo app for smartphones.

The whole classroom was then consolidated with a one-day workshop designed to prepare them finally for the actual exam they were due to take.

Outcomes

Using the four levels of evaluation.

Level 1

Level 1, did they enjoy it? We sought anecdotal evidence from the learners when they attended the revision workshops. They enjoyed the Prezis. They liked specifically the trainer video clips with the trainer and flip charts. They liked the lighthearted nature of the delivery and the wide variety of methods contained within the videos.

They liked the ability to watch anywhere on any device, particularly the Generation Y's.

They didn't like monotony, i.e., when the trainer selected only a few elements of multimedia and tried to emulate PowerPoint in the Prezi. Death by PowerPoint bullets also kill in Prezi; this system was never designed for that. Comments from learners stated they didn't like being spoken at.

They liked being included as if the trainer spoke to them directly and acted as the conductor in an orchestra, introducing the various parts of the virtual classroom.

They liked lightheartedness, not too serious, a good mix.

Level 2

Level 2 evaluations, had they learnt anything? The results of the exams came through immediately, and the pass rate was exceptional for the majority. Naturally they had to do their own study as well as enjoy the virtual classrooms and work hard revising prior to the exam.

Level 3

Level 3, any change in behaviour at work? Too soon to gauge this as the exams were designed to keep them in their current jobs, not to further their roles. However, more knowledge gives more confidence, which means better customer service. This just needs to be measured.

Level 4

Level 4, an impact on the bottom line. The way we measured the return on investment was to show two figures.

The first was the cost saving compared with traditional classroom courses.

Here's the cost saving for just one subject. Five hundred staff would have attended six times whole week courses for the six topics. Average of twelve people per course would mean putting on forty courses across the UK at a cost per week, including hire of hotel, lunches, the trainer's time of £7.500 per course—that's £300,000 per subject. Opportunity cost of the learner being out of the office for a whole week compared with being in and available to do selling for much of the day, estimated loss of income of £1,000 per learner, i.e., £500,000, but difficult to pin down.

Compared to virtual classrooms and one revision day. Revision days, same cost, £1,500 per day, so, that's £60,000 for the courses plus opportunity cost of £100,000. Development costs, software costs, equipment costs to produce and upload virtual classrooms, approximately £10,000 per virtual classroom. Peanuts in comparison.

A grand saving per subject of £640,000 multiplied by six subjects equals an awful big saving.

The second was the return on investment for the company, i.e., keeping 500 people in the situation earning profits, not being fined by the regulator, and not having to recruit new staff to replace the ones they already had. If they all passed their exams, existing staff were qualified to advise customers.

Final reflection

in the opposite direction.

Professors up in arms over online learning

NYMag.com
(New York)

Are MOOCs the future of American education? President Obama hinted as much in a recent speech, says Jonathan Chait, and the very prospect is enraging many US college professors. MOOC stands for "massive open online course", which basically means teaching undergraduates wholly, or partly, through the internet. As Obama put it, at a time when college fees are going up 6% or 7% a year, blending teaching with online learning may help make the system more affordable. Many academics are appalled: you can't teach people en masse remotely, they cry; education requires face-to-face contact. But is an online lesson so different from attending a lecture in a vast auditorium? What really bothers the critics is the thought of MOOCs prompting colleges to cut down staff numbers. That's a real prospect, but we can't design "a higher education system around maintaining living standards for college professors". The interests of students have to come first. To insist that the traditional teaching is "the only way a student ought to be able to get a degree, in an economy where a college degree is necessary for a middle-class life, is to doom the children of non-affluent families to crushing college debt, or to lock them out of upward mobility altogether".

THE WEEK 10 August 2013